CHASING
THE PROMISES
OF AN AWESOME
GOD

BY RUTH CHASE

Printed in the United States of America
World Trade Printing Company
Print Media Books
Garden Grove CA 92841
ISBN 978-1-936510-06-1
First printing April 2015

Back cover photo by Jerusha Schoenhoff

Dedication

This book is dedicated to my loving and patient husband Frederick Thomas Chase, my dearest friend and the love of my life. He made it so easy for me to serve God. He continually encouraged me to do speaking engagements, to lead Bible studies, to present slides of our missions' travels, and to give generously as God led us.

But they that wait upon the Lord
shall renew their strength;
they shall mount up with wings as eagles;
they shall run, and not be weary;
and they shall walk, and not faint.

Isaiah 40:31

To all who read this book:

God will not fail those who wait on the Lord and trust His guidance. His grace shall be sufficient for them. They shall have strength to labor, strength to resist, strength to bear. They shall rise up as eagles in the sky, with wings that strongly and swiftly lift them heavenward. They shall walk and run the way of God's commandments, cheerfully, and with perseverance. They shall not faint and therefore in due season, they shall reap.

Ps 119:105
Thy word is a lamp
unto my feet, and a
light unto my path
God Bless
Ruth Chase

Acknowledgements

Many thanks to Scott and Sandi Tompkins, my longtime friends, who were willing to accept the task of helping me with my manuscript despite their busy schedule. Scott spent many hours lovingly laboring to enhance the stories with his editorial skills. Thanks too to Sandi for further polishing the manuscript when Scott had finished it. I couldn't have done it without you.

I deeply appreciate my dear friend and co-worker Madge Pike who kept encouraging me to write this book. For years I heard: "Ruth, when are you going to write that book?" I'm grateful Madge for all your help in making this book possible. Your encouragement and practical assistance were invaluable.

I'm also thankful to Yolanda and Roxanne Olson and to Shirley Mariacher for all the many hours they spent typing the stories. I appreciate Carole Birong for motivating me to actually start my book in January 2014. These friends not only helped me write this, but also supported me in prayer. I'm especially thankful for the prayer support of Mary Shin, my friend from Korea.

I can't complete this list without giving highest praise and thanks to God. He gave me a wonderful Mom and Dad, a good family, and a fine husband who were always there for me. Without the Lord, none of these things would have ever happened. There would be no story. So glory be to our awesome God who has made all this possible.

Ruth Chase

Foreword

Ruth Chase – One amazing woman

As I have journeyed through life I have met many wonderful and distinguished people, including famous actors, presidents, and royalty, but few have made as big an impression on me as Ruth Chase.

I met Ruth and her late husband, Fred, soon after they came to Youth With A Mission (YWAM) in Kona in 1992. We had in common that we were both from Pennsylvania, the first of many connections. Though Ruth was older than me, I was amazed how spry she was. Daily I would see her hurrying around the campus. She and Fred had a car but she always preferred to walk, often covering several miles a day.

When I first met Ruth I was working in Computer Services at YWAM's University of the Nations. As I helped people on the campus with their computer needs, I would often hear how hard she and Fred worked, especially from Ruth's supervisor, Community Relations Director Ken Clewett. Fred had built all the bookcases in the library, along with most of the dorm furniture on campus. When Ken died a few years later, I knew Ruth would need a new place to serve, so I invited her to help in the Library.

She told me she had no computer experience and did not wish to start learning at this late stage. I told her this would be no problem, as I needed someone to do inventory, and she was willing. While working she would share her stories of God working in her life. They were so uplifting, I required the library staff to get together every Thursday to hear her "God stories." Ruth encouraged us so much with how God had used her and was continuing to use her that I insisted she record these stories so they would not be lost.

Ruth's life is like that of the saints I had read about in that she has full-heartedly served God in all she's done. She is always seeking God's will and walking in it. She's also the most giving person I know. She gives of her time, her energy, her wisdom, and her finances whenever and wherever the Lord leads.

In Revelation 12:11 it tells us how the enemy of God is defeated: "And they overcame Him by the blood of the Lamb, and by the word of their testimony; and they loved not their lives unto the death." To me this describes Ruth, her life and this book. She was saved by the blood of the Lamb and works with God daily to spread the Good News – not just in word but in actions. She testifies to the goodness of God in all she does and is willing to do so as long as she has breath.

May all who read this book gain knowledge and acceptance of the goodness of God in their lives too.

Madge Bridges Pike
Library Director
University of the Nations
Kailua Kona, Hawaii

Table of Contents

First Steps of Faith

Trusting God for my future

As I look back on my long life, I can see so well the timing of God. I didn't always recognize it, yet I have had a sense His hand was on me at all times.

I was the youngest of five daughters born to Ora Benjamin and Carrie Rebecca Hepler on September 16, 1928, near Fryburg, Pennsylvania. I grew up in the country in a good home where I was taught to live a respectable, moral life: don't lie, don't cheat, don't steal, etc. I followed that code of honesty, but I remember at an early age I feared dying. I believed in God and in heaven and hell, yet I still wasn't sure where I was headed.

One thing I knew for certain was that the Bible was the Word of God. Based on Bible verses I had read, I realized I was a sinner and not fit for heaven:

- "For all have sinned, and come short of the glory of God" (Romans 3:23).
- "...Verily, verily I say unto thee, Except a man be born again, he cannot see the kingdom of God" (John 3:3).
- "For by grace are ye saved through faith; and that not of yourselves: it is the gift of God; Not of works lest any man should boast" (Ephesians: 2:8-9).
- "For God so loved the world, that He gave His only begotten Son, that whosoever believeth in Him should not perish, but have everlasting life" (John 3:16).

In my teen years, I began hungering to know God and came to recognize that I hadn't yet received God's gift of grace. Thank God, I repented of my sins and accepted Christ as my Savior at a Kathryn Kuhlman meeting at the age of 17. I soon began praying that others in my family would come to know Jesus. God began answering my prayers. Several in my family were saved and some of those went into the ministry.

My parents taught us early on to work hard, and I got my first paid job at the age of 14, taking care of a 6-year-old girl and helping her mother with cooking and cleaning. My salary was $5 a week. Two years later, I got a job at a jewelry store. During the school year, I worked on Saturdays and in the summer I earned $14 a week.

When I graduated from high school, I needed a full-time job. I learned the A&P grocery store paid $33 a week. So I asked God to give me *that* job. When I went in to inquire, the manager said he did not need anyone at the time. I was disappointed but accepted the answer.

A couple of days later he called and said, "Come in. I am hiring you."

I knew God had given me that job! Later, I learned that the assistant manager had asked the manager if I was looking for a job.

"Yes, she asked if we were hiring."

"Well, if you don't hire her, when you go on vacation I will."

I worked at the A&P store for 28½ years. As Psalm 34:8 says, "O taste and see that the Lord is good: blessed is the man that trusteth in Him."

Praying for a husband

We need to be careful what we pray for because God answers prayer in specific ways. I asked God to give me a husband who did not drink or smoke. God gave me a wonderful husband, one who did not drink or smoke, but at the time he wasn't a Christian. I married Fred Chase on April 10, 1949. He was an industrious, faithful man who was shaped by the lean times of the Great Depression and service in World War II. He built our first home without having to borrow a penny. If we needed something, we did without until we saved the money and could pay cash for it.

God says in 2 Corinthians 6:14, "Be ye not unequally yoked together with unbelievers ... " I wish I had prayed more specifically for a strong *Christian* husband. For the first 12 years of our marriage we went to church, but didn't have Christ at the center of our marriage. My own spiritual life was weak in those years. Our church lacked good Bible teaching, and I found myself drifting. Away from God I was miserable. When my marriage began to fail, I cried unto the Lord: "Forgive me for turning away from You Lord, I need You."

God did forgive me and in March of 1962, He gave me a new heart and a fresh start. I prayed earnestly for Fred to receive Christ too. And to my joy, God saved my husband and our marriage.

Fred had lived a good life so I was concerned he wouldn't recognize his need for Jesus. When I said to him, "I thought you would not know you were lost," he said, "I knew it all the time."

When we committed our marriage to God, Joshua 24:15 instructed us: " ... Choose you this day whom ye will serve ... but as for me and my house, we will serve the LORD."

Put Christ first if you want your marriage to last. I came home one night from work, and Fred was reading his Bible.

"Do you believe the Bible?" he asked.

"Yes, I do."

"It says the man is to be the head of the house."

Need I say anything else?

In July of that year I came to another crisis in my life. The Lord was purifying me, and I recognized how often I was failing God. You can't make Jesus the Lord of your life until you come to the end of yourself and surrender all to Him. One day I was so sick of "self," I finally surrendered all to Jesus. In Romans 12:1, God tells us to present our bodies a living sacrifice. I yielded myself and prayed, "Lord take me, use me, do whatever you want with me." I gave Him everything that day: myself, my possessions, my bank account, my all.

Romans 8 mentions the Holy Spirit 21 times. We must step out of the "self" life into a Spirit-filled life, that the Holy Spirit may control and empower us to live above the world, our flesh, and the devil. Galatians 2:20 says, "I am crucified with Christ: nevertheless I live; yet not I, but Christ liveth in me: and the life which I now live in the flesh I live by the faith of the Son of God, who loved me, and gave Himself for me."

To defeat SIN, remove the 'I' and replace it with an 'O' for SON. Victory is in Jesus. Jeremiah 18:6 (NASB) says, "... like the clay in the potter's hand, so are you in My hand..." Let God have your life. He can do more with it than you can. We all want to run our lives. If we surrender, we are afraid of what He may want us to do; but fear not, He will equip us. He will give us all the ability and tools we need.

Almost immediately God began to use me. My pastor asked if I would be his assistant Sunday School teacher. Not feeling qualified, I replied, "I can't, and I won't." God's voice was like thunder when He chided me, "For what I have done for you, and you don't want to serve Me!"

I quickly answered, "I can't, but with Your help I will," recalling the Apostle Paul's words in Philippians 4:13: "I can do all things through Christ which strengtheneth me."

I became the teacher and taught for 12 years. In 1975 when I quit working, I told the Lord I had extra time to serve Him. He said to quit teaching my Sunday school class, and I did. Then He gave me opportunity to lead eight Bible studies a week for senior citizens. I taught for 15 years without missing a meeting. I led one home Bible study, but the others required driving. Three were 25 miles round trip; four were 65 miles round trip.

God's comfort in times of loss

In my 68 years as a Christian, I have failed God but He has never failed me. He is always there to comfort, strengthen, guide, and meet my every need. His grace is always sufficient. Proverbs 3:5-6 says, "Trust in the LORD with all thine heart; and lean not unto thine own understanding. In all thy ways acknowledge Him, and He shall direct thy paths." God is awesome, and He has directed my life in good times and bad. I love to write about His love and blessings, His goodness and mercies, in all seasons of life.

The year 1962 was a great time of blessing for Fred and me. He gave his heart to the Lord, and I came to the end of "self" and surrendered my will to the Holy Spirit. These changes brought new joy and peace and holiness to our daily lives. Holiness isn't how much we have of God, but how much God has of us. That same eventful year, my father died at the age of 69. I had gone to see him and mom just a couple days before his death. On my way home I stopped at the local funeral home as my cousin had died and I wanted to pay my respects. When I signed the register I saw my father's name. I suddenly knew he would be next to die. So when the phone rang with the news of my father's passing, I was somewhat prepared. I remember a lot of nice things about my father. I loved to hear him play the harmonica and clog dance. I fondly remembered him singing *When the Roll is Called Up Yonder, I'll be There.* Now he was there.

The Lord took care of mother in this time of need. She had

started receiving her Social Security just seven months before. The Kern family, who my father had worked for, had a building with apartments in Oil City. They gave mother an apartment for $5 a month. Mother lived 20 years after my father's death and couldn't have had her own apartment but for the generosity of the Kerns. Mother would always say, "God promises to take care of the widows, and He sure takes care of me." Mother's Bible had all the verses underlined that spoke of the widow.

In 1977 my mother was told she had a rare growth which was cancer in the liver and gallbladder duct. She had surgery at Cleveland Clinic. They were unable to get the roots so when it grew back, they did a bypass. She spent another 30 days in Cleveland Clinic. Fred's father had a massive heart attack at the same time and was in the Pittsburgh hospital. Somehow, I managed to keep leading the eight Bible studies each week, while always finding time for my mom. Once a week I took care of her needs and cleaned her house. By this time she lived in a high rise.

In February 1982 mother said she wanted to make a quilt. I said, "Mother you don't want to be making a quilt in the summer." She answered, "I won't... it will be finished by that time." Sure enough, by the middle of April, the fabric was ready for the church ladies to quilt. No sooner had I dropped the material off at the church, I had to take my mother to the doctor. She was jaundiced and was admitted to the hospital. For six weeks the family took turns staying with mother around the clock. Everyone said to me, "You better slow down or you will have a nervous breakdown." I just kept going. God is my strength.

Mother got her wish. We kept the apartment until she died, and she was able to see her quilt completed. She gave it to me for assisting her so much, but I knew when she was making it, she had intended that it go to Carrie, a great granddaughter who was named for her. Since I already had four quilts, I was pleased to give it to Carrie who is also my great niece.

For five years Mother never had a day without pain. But she didn't complain. Only once did she say, "If God isn't going to heal me, I wish He would take me home."

She died the day before Memorial Day, at 9:25 a.m. Sunday, May 30, 1982. Fred's dad died that evening at 10:45 p.m. They both had been sick for five years. Their funeral services were the same day: Mother's at 11:00 a.m. in Oil City; Fred's dad at 2:00 p.m. about 30 miles away in Clintonville, Pennsylvania.

Mother came from a generation that sacrificially did without to give to her children. She was grateful, selfless, and a peacemaker, always content. Such contentment is priceless. With Fred's dad and my mom being sick at the same time, many opportunities arose to witness of God's goodness and how He was meeting their needs and ours.

Over those years I had many occasions to speak throughout Venango County Pennsylvania in churches, Rotary Clubs, Lion Clubs, the Emlenton men's prayer breakfasts, and local mother-daughter banquets. These times brought me great joy. I loved telling "God stories" and sometimes showing slides of our international mission travels. When I spoke to women I taught from 2 Timothy 1:5 about Timothy's mother, Eunice, and his grandmother, Lois, and the importance of being a godly mother and grandmother.

One of the most memorable events was a Valentine's Day at a Senior Citizen Center when I shared about love. When we think of Valentine's Day we think of those who are dear to our hearts and how we can show our love to them. Many give flowers or a box of candy. As children we learn to send cards or little notes on

Valentine's Day. But God says love is more!

Luke 6:32, 35 says: "For if ye love them which love you, what thank have ye? For sinners also love those that love them ... But love ye your enemies, and do good, and lend, hoping for nothing again; and your reward shall be great, and ye shall be the children of the Highest: for He is kind unto the unthankful and to the evil."

I wanted to challenge those senior citizens to love more fully as God loves us. I told them of how my husband Fred understood that love was more than just words. After being married several years, I said to him one day, "You never tell me you love me anymore."

The Chases celebrate 50 years of marriage.

"Don't I show you by what I do?" he replied.

"Yes, you do."

Love is doing, but it's good to hear the words again. Maybe Fred was like another man I heard about. When his wife reminded him that he never told her he loved her, he replied, "I told you once, and if I ever change my mind, I'll let you know."

The Bible shows that love finds its expression in service to our fellow men and is the chief test of Christian discipleship. Love is proved by service. An example is in the book of Ruth: When her mother-in-law Naomi was leaving the land of Moab, Ruth said,

"Entreat me not to leave thee, or to return from following after thee; for whither thou goest, I will go, and where thou lodgest, I will lodge. Thy people shall be my people, and thy God, my God" (Ruth 1:16, KJ21®).

This is love in words. Ruth gleaned in the fields of Boaz to support her mother-in-law. At the end of the first day she not only took home the barley she had gleaned, but also she had saved part of her lunch. That was love in action.

Ruth was easy to love since Naomi loved her, but God challenges us to love our enemies also. He tells us how in 1 Corinthians 13, which is known as the love chapter:

"Love is patient and kind; love is not jealous or boastful; it is not arrogant or rude. Love does not insist on its own way; it is not irritable or resentful; it does not rejoice at wrong, but rejoices in the right. Love bears all things, believes all things, hopes all things, endures all things ... So faith, hope, love abide, these three; but the greatest of these is love" (1 Corinthians 13:4-7, 13, RSV).

The eternal search of mankind is to love and be loved. The ultimate of love, however, is to know God's love in our lives. Christian love outshines all. In John 13:34 Jesus said, "A new commandment I give unto you, That ye love one another; as I have loved you, that ye also love one another."

The Great Commandment in Luke 10:27 says, "Thou shalt love the Lord thy God with all thy heart, and with all thy soul, and with all thy strength, and with all thy mind; and thy neighbor as thyself."

Can we respond in love to those who are not loving to us? Not only on Valentine's Day, but every day of the year.

The Clock of Life[1]

The clock of life is wound but once
And no man has the power
To tell just when the hands will stop
At late or early hour.
Now is the only time we own
Live, love, toil with a will.
Do not wait until tomorrow
For the clock may then be still.

I have seen too many people stopped cold by discouragement. It's the devil's favorite tool in thwarting the work of God. Whatever trials we encounter, we cannot be separated from the love of God (Romans 8:38-39). We may turn from Him, but He will never turn from us.

In the book of Genesis, Joseph could have given up on life. He was betrayed and sold into slavery by his brothers; he was falsely accused and sent to prison; his plea for release was never heard. Yet, he didn't dissolve in self-pity or bitterness. He kept working faithfully wherever he was. And one day God elevated him beyond anything he could have hoped for.

I once encountered a young man who was not chosen for a staff position he wanted. He wanted to quit, but I challenged him to keep doing the work God had given him and to do it well. Every time I saw him I asked how things were going and encouraged him in his work. A year later, God gave him the position he had prayed for.

Don't waste the time God has given you.

---

1. This poem is attributed to many people. The earliest copyright indicates the author is Wilfred Grindle Conary, although Robert H. Smith is frequently credited as well as Anonymous.

11

Where Jesus Walked

A dream come true

After my oldest brother, Clinton, accepted Christ as his Savior, he gave Bibles to me and my two older sisters, Twila and Beulah. I was 13 years old at the time I received mine, and this Bible was a special treasure for me. I still have it today, although it no longer has a front or back cover.

For many years, as I read this Bible, I would look at the maps contained in the back pages to see the various places where Jesus was born, where he lived and traveled, and all the wonderful places described in the Word. I developed a great longing to visit these places and see them for myself. As I grew up, it became my heart's desire to go to Israel.

I thought of the words in the Bible: "Delight thyself also in the LORD: and He shall give thee the desires of thine heart. Commit thy way unto the LORD; trust also in Him; and He shall bring it to pass" (Psalm 37:4-5).

I heard that Frances and Ruben McCandless from Grove City were going to take a tour to Israel and Europe with Dr. Torrey Johnson, the founder of Youth for Christ. It was scheduled for Easter season, April 4 to 25, 1966. My husband Fred knew of my dream and had encouraged me to pursue it. So upon hearing of this tour, I signed up to join it.

At one Wednesday night prayer meeting in church, God spoke to me very clearly. He told me that I was to take picture slides of my trip and show them to others on my return. I did not own a camera at the time. I had not taken a single photo in my life, but obediently, I purchased a Canon Sure Shot camera and took it with me.

Upon arrival at the Pittsburgh airport, I was happily surprised to see my old friend Pearl Gibbons in the waiting area. She was taking the same tour, and we became roommates for the trip.

Once in New York City, we checked in at the Alitalia Air Lines where we joined the rest of the group including Dr. Johnson. The 41 of us on this tour included seven nurses and one doctor. I thought to myself, *well, if anyone in the group becomes ill, they would certainly have good care.* As it turned out, the one physician was an eye doctor.

Wayne Thomas, our soloist, made the rounds and gave his testimony to each person individually. He said he used to sing in nightclubs, but had dedicated his voice now for the glory of the Lord.

Our tour made stops in Milan and Rome, Italy, before flying on to the Mideast. On one flight, I remember sitting beside a friendly young man from Greece. As we began to converse, he told me he had no religion of any kind. I told him about how God had transformed my life, and I gave him some gospel tracts that I carried with me. He said he would read them and share them with his wife.

Leaving Rome on Jordanian Airlines, I found myself seated next to a geologist. He also was not a believer and told me he was headed to Amman, Jordan, to work on a water exploration project. I told him that I hoped he could find the water source he was looking for, but also that he would find the Living Water—Jesus! I always pray that God will have me sit beside someone who needs Him.

From the city of Amman, we boarded another plane to Cairo,

Egypt where a tour bus awaited us. As Pearl and I sat on our tour bus, I looked out the window and saw a man standing by the Nile River holding a bucket in his hand. The river looked muddy and dirty, and yet I saw him scoop up river water and go sit on a bench nearby. He retrieved a loaf of bread from his satchel, broke off a piece and dipped it in the bucket and ate it. This was shocking to me. If I were to do the same thing, I would probably get sick and die of contamination.

Our bus driver, Zag, proved to be quite a jokester. During that tour, we stopped and mounted a rather interesting conveyance—a camel! Mounting the camel was an adventure in itself. The camel would lie down on its knees and we hopped on its back that way. It was vital to hold on tight to the saddle as the camel lifted up its haunches and tipped us forward. It would have been easy to fly forward and over the animal's head during this time. This was truly a novel journey, clopping along the sandy trail on these large animals, to view the giant pyramids and see the Sphinx. When camels walk, they sway from one side

Easter service in 1966 at the Garden Tomb in Jerusalem

to the other. Then, getting ready to dismount, I gripped the saddle tightly when the camels front legs dropped down to kneel, pushing me forward until his back end also dropped down and I could climb off. I was very careful to keep a good distance from the camel's head, because they are continuously slobbering and have been known to spit on bystanders.

We flew by Caravelle jet from Cairo to Jordan where Rev. Allison, a Christian Missionary Alliance (CMA) missionary, met us. The next day, we toured the Mount of Olives where Christ ascended to heaven and where He will return again someday. Then, Rev. Allison led us to the Garden of Gethsemane. He said some of the gnarled olive trees there are believed to have been alive as Jesus prayed to the Father, "Not my will, but Thine, be done" Luke 22:42). From the garden, we could easily gaze over the Kidron Valley to see the Golden Gate through which Christ passed triumphantly on Palm Sunday on the borrowed foal of a donkey. We saw too, the place where Stephen was stoned, and walked through Stephen's Gate to see the Via Dolorosa. From there, we went to Bethlehem where Christ was born.

Our tour was just a year before the Six-Day War in 1967, and at the time Jerusalem was ruled by Jordan. Tensions between Arabs and Jews were high, yet the Old City seemed alive with activity. The caretaker at the Garden Tomb was a Christian Arab. He told us he had been a wealthy landowner, but the Jews had confiscated his lands. He took this job to help support his wife and eight children. "As a result of this job, I've met Christ in a new way." He shared his testimony with us of knowing he is being used of the Lord to win many souls as he tells the story of the risen Christ at the Garden tomb. He told us he would have been willing to give up his riches long ago if he had known the rewards of walking close with the Lord.

We also went to see Golgotha, referred to as "the place of the skull." Our bus rolled on through the Judean Hills and countryside to Jericho and the Dead Sea. I have good memories of all of us singing gospel hymns each time we traveled in the bus. Jericho surprised me with its beauty. Located 1,200 feet below sea level, the climate is semi-tropical. The Dead Sea, at 1,300 feet below sea level, is the lowest spot in the world. There are no life forms in the Dead Sea because of the high salt content. We also visited the Jordan River and the place believed to be where John the Baptist baptized Jesus. The Jordan has become a popular place for tourists to get baptized or re-baptized.

On April 10,1966—Resurrection Sunday—we all met for breakfast and were pleasantly surprised when our waiters served us pretty colored Easter eggs along with the familiar, "Happy Easter!" greeting. At ten o'clock, we all gathered at the Garden Tomb where Dr. Johnson led a special Resurrection service for us. I estimated there were over a thousand people at the tomb that morning. Even today, I cannot describe what it was like to be right there where Christ was buried and rose from the dead!

The Christian and Missionary Alliance has been sending missionaries to Jerusalem since the 1890s. Two CMA missionaries, who had served there for many years trying to reach Muslims with the Gospel, also conducted an Easter service. In our conversation with them, we learned that they needed a car to help with their ministry. Suddenly, it all came together for me as God spoke to my heart that morning. He told me that when I returned home, I was to share my photos of the trip, and the freewill offerings collected were to help the missionaries purchase a new vehicle.

Leaving the Garden Tomb, our group went through the Damascus Gate to the Dome of the Rock, a Muslim shrine built on the place where Abraham is believed to have gone to sacrifice his son Isaac, as an offering to God.

We continued on to see the ancient Wailing Wall, where Jews pray for the Messiah and for the rebuilding of the temple in Jerusalem, and later prayed ourselves at a site purported to be the Upper Room, where Jesus washed the feet of His disciples.

At the Book of the Shrine Museum, we saw the Dead Sea Scrolls including the complete book of Isaiah. From the bus we saw Mount Tabor, the Mount of Transfiguration, Mount Carmel and the Valley of Megiddo (believed to be the location of Armageddon where there will be a great battle just prior to the second advent of Christ).

Our guide often mentioned the fruitfulness of Israel, and said the land is getting greener every year due to expanded irrigation. The country now produces bananas, cherries, date palms, and olive and pomegranate trees. As prophesied in Isaiah 35:1, there are also fields of hay and wheat growing. Near Nazareth I planted a tree for only $2. It seemed to be a small contribution, but I left there feeling I am part of the greening of Israel and a scriptural fulfillment. There have been millions of trees planted in the decades since I was there, and it's beautiful to see the effect it is having on this once desolate land.

Day after day, site after site, the Bible was coming to life in my heart. We visited Tiberius and the place where Christ preached the Sermon on the Mount. It was interesting to experience the acoustics in that natural amphitheater, while imagining how the people at that time would hear Jesus speak one of the most heralded sermons in history.

Crossing the Sea of Galilee was another highlight. On this lake many centuries ago, Jesus had shocked His followers by walking calmly to their fishing boat in the midst of the rough waves and storm. Upon seeing his master, Peter zealously stepped from the boat to meet Christ. However, it became necessary for Jesus to grasp Peter's hand when he became fearful and started to sink.

Our guides continued their narration as we crisscrossed the country in the bus. As I packed my suitcase to return from the Holy Land, I felt warm and fulfilled to have seen all these wonderful sights. I had done what most people who come to this sacred land want to do. I had walked where Jesus walked, and in doing so, I felt closer to Him than ever before. I also had divine encounters along the way in which I was able to share my faith freely with those who needed the message of Christ. Even on our flight home, as we flew to Istanbul, I was able to witness to two Jewish men.

After flying to Izmir, the ancient biblical city of Smyrna, we took a bus to Ephesus, the city visited by Paul on his second and third missionary journeys. The city had a centuries-old amphitheater, and our worship leader, Wayne Thomas, found the acoustics to be perfect. He sang a marvelous rendition of "How Great Thou Art" and other favorites like "There's Room at the Cross" and "It Took a Miracle." Dr. Johnson preached an inspiring sermon from the book of Ephesians, and especially stressed the verses with "walk" in them. This highlighted how we should live and walk in our Christian life. Ephesus is the first church spoken of in the Book of Revelation. God had warned the church to repent or their candlestick would be removed, and this is what has happened.

The next leg of our journey was flying to Athens, Greece. We stood on Mars Hill below the Acropolis, where Paul preached about the unknown God. Leaving there we took the hour-and-a-half bus trip along the Mediterranean Sea to Corinth. On the return we landed once again in Rome and went to Vatican City.

We marveled at the Sistine Chapel with its priceless murals by Michelangelo. Upon entering St. Peter's Basilica, we found a vantage point from which we had a spectacular view of St. Peter's Square. We also saw Mamertine Prison, which was possibly the final place of confinement for the Apostle Paul. Our bus driver took us to the catacombs where the first Christians buried their dead and where they were forced to hide in times of persecution.

We then flew to Paris where we were able to visit the Louvre Museum, home to the classic Mona Lisa portrait by Leonardo Da Vinci. I had not heard the instruction given to the tour group not to photograph the painting. I whipped out my camera and took a photo of it. The others in the group pulled me aside and said it was a big No-No!

Like thousands of other tourists, we visited Notre Dame Cathedral and rode the elevator up the 984 feet in the Eiffel Tower. What a magnificent view of the city! In England we visited Stratford-upon-Avon, where Shakespeare came to fame, and attended service at Westminster Abbey, where Dr. Martyn Lloyd-Jones preached for one hour to a congregation of 2,000 people.

I loved the beauty of the English countryside, with their warning signs like "Give Way," "Think Before Overtaking," and "Mind the Gap." At Buckingham Palace someone jokingly told us that the Palace's high-security fence wasn't to keep people out, but to keep Prince Phillip in! We had another good laugh at a dog cemetery where one of the tombstones stated, "Here lies my dog Fifi, more faithful than my three husbands."

All too soon, it was time to fly home. Just after take-off, lunch was served onboard our flight. As I bowed my head in prayer, the flight attendant accidentally dropped Pearl's tray on my head. What a mess! I was not hurt, and we had a good laugh while I went to the washroom to clean up. Just that morning, I had told Pearl and Dave and Mary, who were part of our group, that nothing exciting ever happened to me. I guess I spoke too soon!

The seven-hour flight from London Heathrow to JFK International Airport in New York went as scheduled. However, upon arrival we were told that our connecting flight to Pittsburgh had been cancelled. We were told to wait and catch another plane leaving at 9:00 p.m. Even that flight was 45 minutes late in departing. I thought of my family waiting for me in Pittsburgh. They had to wait patiently till our plane finally landed in Pittsburgh about 11:00 p.m. I realized that in the last 25 hours, I had not had any sleep. Even so, I was very happy to see Fred and the others! It was 2:00 a.m. when we finally pulled into our driveway. Thankfully, it didn't take me long to hop in bed and fall fast asleep!

The trip was all I had expected and more. I enjoyed every minute of it. Many people dream of visiting Israel but will never get there. I'm thankful the Lord gave me the opportunity through my slides to give them a tour of places they might never experience personally.

One week after my trip ended, my pastor asked if I was ready to show my slides. As I loaded my slides into the carousel, I received a Scripture for each photo. Somehow I remembered every one of those verses as I showed them in churches and other locations, as many as two or three times a week till December of 1966.

As I prayed for the Zieglers—the two CMA missionaries in Jerusalem—and their need for a car, I trusted God to answer this need by Christmas time. Finally, in a letter from the Zieglers dated December 20th, they told me that because of the gifts from me and others, the new car had been bought and paid for!

In all I counted 105 times and places where I had shared my

presentation, sending all the free will offerings to the Zieglers. Later, they told me I had been the one who sent in the most money. In gratitude, they decided to name their new vehicle, "The Little Chaser."

Truly we serve an awesome and faithful God!

Back to the Holy Land

Seven years had passed since my first trip to Israel in 1966. That trip was a major influence on my personal Bible study and my teaching in Sunday School class.

I so wanted Fred to be able to experience it – to walk where Jesus walked and preached and performed miracles. I described to him Golgotha, the place of the skull, a barren hillside where Jesus was crucified. How moved I was to behold the place where Jesus shed His blood for me and all people. As Romans 5:8 says, "But God commendeth His love toward us in that, while we were yet sinners, Christ died for us."

In 1973 Fred joined me when I returned with this group to Jerusalem.

23

I also wanted Fred to see the Garden Tomb where Jesus was buried and rose again. Having our Easter service there in 1966, stirred in me a joy so overwhelming I can never describe it. I still feel like Paul when he wrote in 2 Corinthians 9:15, "Thanks be unto God for His unspeakable gift."

One year after my first visit, war broke out in the Holy Land. Raids by Palestinian groups based in Lebanon, Syria, and Jordan escalated into what became known as the Six-Day War of 1967. I stayed glued to the TV during those six days. At first, Israel seemed to be losing. Then it launched attacks that destroyed much of the Egyptian and Syrian air forces. Within a week Israel had won, gaining control of Jerusalem, the West Bank, Sinai and the Golan Heights. It was miraculous!

PRAISING GOD
I was so thankful Fred got to experience the Holy Land. On our way home, we visited the Greek cities of Athens (above) and Corinth. Like me, Fred said his view of the Bible would never be quite the same. We arrived home praising God for the wonderful trip to the Holy Land.

Much had changed in the country when I returned with Fred in 1973. Solomon Mattar, a Christian Arab, had been the keeper of the Garden Tomb. He was such a wonderful man with a powerful testimony. He'd been killed in

24

the Garden Tomb area during the war. I loved being back at the tomb, but without Solomon it just didn't feel the same.

I was amazed at how much the landscape of Israel had changed in the few years I'd been away. Trees and gardens were growing everywhere. The whole land was becoming more beautiful!

I thought of Isaiah 35:1 which says, "...the desert shall rejoice and blossom as the rose." Another prophecy in Ezekiel 36:35 says, " ... This land that was desolate is become like the Garden of Eden ... "

Some missionaries told us the story of how the land had become desolate. In Leviticus 26:33, God declared, "And I will scatter you among the heathen, and will draw out a sword after you: and your land shall be desolate, and your cities waste."

The missionaries said God fulfilled this prophecy after the Crusades in the 13th Century. The people were taxed for each tree that was on their land. Rather than pay the high tax demanded by the government, the people cut down the trees. This resulted in severe soil erosion that turned a land once flowing with milk and honey into a wasteland. After Israel won the Six-Day War, they launched major irrigation and reforestation projects.

There were other signs of change. When I first visited the Wailing Wall, which is the only remaining structure of Solomon's Temple, there were rows and rows of little Arab houses built almost up to the wall. This time as we approached the Wailing Wall, I was surprised we could see it from such a distance. Then I realized, all those houses had been removed.

I was so thankful Fred got to experience the Holy Land. On our way home, we also visited the Greek cities of Athens and Corinth. Like me, Fred said his view of the Bible would never be quite the same.

The last tour and the hidden city

Just a year after Fred and I returned from Israel, I learned that Rev. Herbert McComas was planning to lead another Bible Land tour. I had learned so much from him on the previous tour, and when I heard this tour was going to Petra, my heart jumped within me.

I had wanted to see this spectacular hidden city since I first heard about it. Based on my reading of Scripture, I believe it is the place "prepared of God" where Jews will hide to escape the antichrist during the tribulation period (Revelation 12:6).

Fred was unable to go with me this time so I took my nephew Rev. Samuel Tinsley and his wife Lillian. We left Pittsburgh on March 4 and arrived in Amman, Jordan, the next day. Jordan had experienced a severe winter, and there was still snow on the ground in some places. Our tour group set out for Petra, but along the way stopped at two biblical sites. The first was an area of blackened stone described as the possible location of Sodom and Gomorrah, two wicked cities that God destroyed by fire from heaven. We also stopped at a spring, said to be the place where Moses acted in disobedience to God with bitter consequences.

Numbers 20:7-8 says, "And the Lord spake unto Moses, saying, Take the rod, and gather thou the assembly together, thou and Aaron thy brother, and speak ye unto the rock before their eyes; and it shall give forth his water ... " God wanted to witness His power to the rebellious Israelites. Unfortunately Moses was feeling his own frustration with them so he did it his way. Numbers 20:10-11 says, "And Moses and Aaron gathered the congregation together before the rock, and he said unto them, 'Hear now, ye rebels; must we fetch you water out of this rock?' And

Moses lifted up his hand, and with his rod he smote the rock twice: and the water came out abundantly, and the congregation drank, and their beasts also." Note that God want to show His provision (love) for His people, while Moses laid a guilt trip on them. Because of his disobedience, Moses never did enter the Promised Land.

There is responsibility that comes with listening to God. We must heed His word and truly reflect what He wants others to know of His love. *Lord, let my steps and my tongue be yours!* Water still comes out of that rock to this day. Some members of our group were refreshed by its cool spring water.

After several more miles, we came upon a magnificent over-view of Petra, a city carved from rose-red stone. After mounting horses, we started the unforgettable two-mile ride down into Petra which was built by the Nabataeans and flourished from about 30 BC to 300 AD. We entered the deserted city through a deep split in the mountain known as the *Siq*, almost a mile long, but only 10 to 20 feet wide. The walls on either side rose hundreds of feet to the sky.

Emerging from the *Siq*, the first building we saw was an imposing two-story tomb carved from the red canyon wall known as the Treasury of Pharaoh. The walls of the Petra valley contain hundreds of cave openings, many with intricately carved entrances. This place was all I imagined it to be and more.

The next day we traveled to Jericho. As described in Joshua 6, Jericho was a great city surrounded by high walls. The Israelites marched around the city seven times as directed by God. When they blew the trumpets and raised a shout, the Bible says "the wall fell down flat." Jericho is one of the world's oldest cities. Archaeologists have unearthed broken walls and towers there and we got to see some. Scholars say the city was destroyed and rebuilt several times in its long history.

Perhaps the most exciting archaeological discovery of the last century in Israel were the Dead Sea Scrolls, the first found accidentally by a Bedouin shepherd boy in 1946. Over the next decade, thousands of fragments were found in 11 caves. We drove to the Qumran caves where the scrolls were found. These scrolls have been dated back to the Hasmonean Dynasty (142-63 BC) and the early Roman periods (63 BC – 68 AD). They represent every book of the traditional Hebrew canon (the Old Testament), except Esther. Many skeptics of God's Word say that the Bible has gone through so many transliterations that it cannot be accurate or true. The Dead Sea Scrolls show these skeptics to be absolutely wrong. The texts from Qumran proved to be word-for-word identical to our standard Hebrew Bible in more than 95 percent of the text. The 5 percent of variation consisted mostly of spelling alterations.

The scrolls are on display at the Shrine of the Book Museum in Jerusalem. I was surprised and grateful to be able to walk around and study the 24-foot long Scroll of Isaiah, the only biblical book found in its entirety.

We walked to Pilate's Judgment Hall where Christ was condemned to death. John 18:28 says, "Then led they Jesus from Caiaphas unto the hall of judgment: and it was early; and they themselves went not into the judgment hall, lest they should be defiled; but that they might eat the Passover." Marks from the games that the Roman soldiers played were still evident on the courtyard pavement. Some believe this is one thing that is truly authentic in the old city.

While in Jerusalem, I hired a cab to take me and some others to the nearby town of Essawiyha to visit my friend Thamer Essawi and his family. I first met Thamer when he was a student at Grove City College in Pennsylvania. He came to our home many times for dinner. One of those times, I surprised and delighted him with a birthday cake. Before he returned home, he gave me a beautiful red prayer rug, which is still on display in my home.

"It's so good to see you again," Thamer said, embracing me with a strong arm and a warm smile. "This is the woman I told you about, she and her husband Fred showed me much kindness."

Thamer's household welcomed me and my friends as family. It was a joy to meet his parents and to see where he worked as a teacher: Birzeit College, which today is Birzeit University. Thamer spent one day with me in the old city of Jerusalem. He's an Arab and a Muslim so he saw the city in a much different way. I trust that he will one day receive Christ; I have prayed many times for his salvation. I hope Fred and I were good examples of what it is to be Christians. On our last night in Jerusalem I invited him to join me and a friend along with the Zieglers (the CMA missionaries) for dinner at our hotel, a sweet evening of fun, friendship and fellowship.

In Jerusalem I noticed that all the commercial vehicles have the prefix number of 666 on the license plates. I asked the bus driver why. He said: "That's the Israeli peace symbol. It stands for the Six-Day War which started the 6th day of the 6th month." I found this thought-provoking since 666 is also the number of the antichrist described in Revelation 13:18.

We left Jerusalem by bus, bound for Tiberius. Along the way we saw Mt. Gerizim, known as the Mount of Blessing, and Mt. Ebal, the Mount of Cursing. God said to Israel in Deuteronomy 11:29, "And it shall come to pass when the LORD thy God hath brought thee in unto the land whither thou goest to possess it, that thou shalt put the blessing upon mount Gerizim, and the curse upon mount Ebal." Not surprisingly, Mt. Gerizim looked lush and green, but Mt. Ebal was barren.

We also visited Jacob's Well, believed to be where Jesus met the Samaritan woman and asked her for a drink (John 4:5-42). I've heard of many ways to win souls, but this location reminded me of the greatest soul-winner, Jesus, and how He witnessed to His so-called enemies. The Jews had nothing to do with the Samaritans going miles out of their way to avoid them. Even the name was considered a derogative term. But in this scene Jesus reaches across cultural barriers to win her soul.

She asks, "How is it that thou, being a Jew, askest drink of me, which am a woman of Samaria? For the Jews have no dealing with the Samaritans."

Jesus dispelled that argument by saying, "If thou knewest the gift of God, and who it is that saith to thee, Give me to drink; thou wouldest have asked of him, and he would have given thee living water." She posed a religious question about the disagreement between Samaritans and Jews over where to worship. Jesus replied, "...the hour cometh and now is, when the true worshippers shall worship the Father in spirit and in truth..."

In the course of their lengthy conversation, He exposed her sinful life yet did not condemn her. She finally said when Messiah comes "he will tell us all things." Jesus said to her, "I that speak unto thee am He."

The Samaritan woman left her water pot and ran into the city, telling everyone she met about Jesus. "Come, see...Could this be the Messiah?" (John 4:29, NIV). She brought many to Christ. She was one of the first home missionaries. We are all called to be home missionaries. It's impossible to keep the good news of salvation a secret. Proverbs 11:30 says, "he that winneth souls is wise."

Daily we have opportunities to plant the seed of salvation; others will water; and God will give the increase.

On the return journey, we stopped in Athens. We visited the Olympic Stadium, the Royal Palace, the Acropolis and the Parthenon. Then we came to Mars Hill, the place where Paul preached to the Greek intellectuals. In Acts 17 it describes how Paul stood before the believers of many gods and proclaimed the truth of the one true God. He declared God to be the Creator of all things, "For in Him we live, and move, and have our being ... " (v. 28). He urged them to turn from idols and believe in the resurrected Christ. Like Paul, we must be prepared to present the truth in all situations. I was blessed to have my nephew, Rev. Samuel Tinsley, lead devotions on Mars Hill.

The next day we traveled 50 miles to Corinth. This is where Paul was brought to the Bema judgment seat. It made me think of 2 Corinthians 5:10 that Christians "must all appear before the judgment seat of Christ; that every one may receive the things done in his body, according to that he hath done, whether it be good or bad."

I thank God we'll be judged in accordance with His love and grace and mercy.

I returned from the Holy Land with renewed enthusiasm. I will long remember the time spent in the lands of the Bible and the lessons God taught me there.

Mission journeys

Adventures in Ecuador

Our airliner taxied down the runway while Fred and I peered excitedly through the small window. The words of a familiar chorus, "Praise God from whom all blessings flow," echoed in my head. I felt so grateful to God for the privilege of joining a missionary tour to Ecuador—our first-ever trip to South America.

I thought back to the Sunday service at our Christian Missionary Alliance (CMA) church when our pastor announced plans for the trip and welcomed the congregation to participate. The group would be hosted by the radio ministry called Heralding Christ Jesus Blessing (HCJB). Pastor Owens mentioned he had a special interest in visiting the CMA school located next door to HCJB in Quito.

The date was April 13, 1969, and our host, Arthur Foss of HCJB met us in Miami and transported all 36 of us to the New Yorker Hotel. Early next morning we met and introduced ourselves to the rest of the tour group that consisted of people from different parts of the United States. It didn't take long for us to feel bonded with these special folks. That same afternoon, we boarded another plane that flew us to South America.

The city of Quito is just south of the Equator and nestled in a valley high in the Andes Mountains. A passing wave of nausea and dizziness reminded us we were now at 9,500 feet (almost two miles above sea level). The air is much thinner at that altitude so no wonder we were feeling a bit more weary than usual!

While driving to the HCJB mission station, our driver pointed out interesting sights along the way. Ecuador is about the size of Colorado and like that state, is mostly mountainous. We especially liked seeing the native Indian people dressed in their various tribal costumes. The mission compound itself is owned and operated by World Radio Missionary Fellowship in Florida, but also serves as home of HCJB in South America.

Walking around the grounds, our tour guides, Lala and Joe Christopher, explained the outreach strategy and broadcasting tools used to send the gospel to people in over 15 languages; people who might possibly never hear the message of Christ through any other means. Seekers have heard and responded to Christ after listening to the gospel message proclaimed on the radio network and have written the station to confirm this.

Each department has four to six workers for each language division. Fred and I were most impressed with the print shop that provided biblical literature to the masses. During the tour, a staff member shared with the group the need to purchase an IBM typesetter machine. They had been renting one, and he said if they had $750 cash, they could use that amount as a down payment, and the rental fees they had been paying each month would instead go toward the purchase price of this valuable piece of equipment.

Just before leaving the print shop, the manager turned to me and asked if I would be willing to pray for them and their need. I bowed my head and began to pray, when I finished I heard God speak to me clearly, "You can do it!" I had a sense of faith and courage well up in my heart as I looked forward to sharing in the answer to this need.

A precious German couple hosted Fred and me during our stay in Quito. However, each evening we would dine with other HCJB staff and this afforded us the chance to get to know some of the other missionaries. During our afternoon times, we ate lunch in the city then went exploring to learn more about the culture.

One afternoon, I decided to show off my one Spanish word at a local restaurant. After our waiter served us, I said to him, "Gracias," meaning thank you. I must have said it well enough because immediately, the waiter began speaking out a barrage of Spanish words that left me sitting there wide-open mouthed. When he finished, I dropped my head and answered meekly, "I no speak Spanish." Was my face red as we paid the check and left the premises! "I guess that should teach me a lesson," I told Fred as we went out the front door.

During one of the tours, our two busloads traveled to the outskirts of town where we came to a vehicle checkpoint. This turned into a one-hour delay while our bus drivers held a lively dialogue with the government officials. Neither bus driver had the required operator license needed to travel in the country-side. I am not quite sure how the situation was resolved, but after returning to the base we were told the bus drivers had to spend the night in jail.

I was continually amazed at the heavy loads of responsibility placed on young children, as they were required to care for even younger siblings every day. At times they even helped care for livestock to protect them from robbers. Without this assistance, it would be difficult for their parents to work and earn even a meager living.

The men worked hard on their land plowing the soil using handcrafted plows they had fashioned for this work, while the women cooked, sewed and washed the laundry by hand in the running streams. When I saw women carrying heavy loads on their backs, I was reminded that in many parts of the world this is a common sight. Sad to say, women are still almost consid-ered beasts of burden in parts of the world. Thankfully, with the entrance of Christianity, women have now been elevated to a higher standard.

About 2.5 hours from the capital city of Quito, we found the famed Saquisili market, and our senses climbed to their highest point. We delighted in seeing beautiful displays of fresh fruits, vegetables, and baskets of bread, grains and sugar cakes. We breathed deeply of the aromatic spices filling the air, not to men-tion the head of a pig roasting on a spit. We heard the clucking of chickens and the loud bleating of sheep that were tied together in the back of a truck. We had heard that the Ecuadorian people were fine artisans, and their love for color and beauty was vividly on display in their hand-loomed tapestries and also the painted

designs on their vehicles. I bought several paintings of the Andes that still hang in my home.

The best preparation we could have had for this journey was reading *Through Gates of Splendor* by Elisabeth Elliot. The story tells of five Mission Aviation Fellowship (MAF) men who flew deep into the jungles of Ecuador in 1956 to minister to the Auca, one of the most war-like tribes in Ecuador.

When their plane landed on a river bank by an Auca village, the tribe attacked and killed missionaries Nate Saint, Jim Elliot, Ed McCully, Roger Youderian, and Peter Fleming.

That incident has gone down in the annals of mission history and thankfully did not end there. Rachel Saint, the sister of Nate, returned to the jungles to minister to the very tribesmen who had murdered her brother and loved ones. She befriended Dayuma, an Auca woman who had escaped from the tribe, and it was Dayuma who taught Rachel how to speak their language.

Rachel, her family and others joined in the quest to lead the Auca people to Christ. Together, they were able to see all the murderers, and over 100 of the villagers become Christian believers. I can't begin to tell you how surprising and special it was for Fred and me now to meet Marge Saint, the widow of Nate Saint, and their sons Steve and Phil. After Nate's death, Marge married the President of HCJB and continued working in Ecuador.

One of our memorable outings was to the town of Pifo, 15 miles east of Quito. I will never forget our journey there. We boarded an old bus adapted to serve as a train car. The scary thing was that the only way to stop this "train" was to turn the wheels in the opposite direction. There were no brakes. Throughout the trip we heard the horn beeping as the driver tried to warn livestock, dogs and children to "clear off the tracks!"

Once we arrived at the Pifo train station, we met a small team of missionary couples and visited their simple brick homes. They were in charge of running the HCJB transmitter facility. We discovered HCJB workers do receive a salary for their work. However, we also found out that from the president on down, they all receive the <u>same</u> salary. The folks we met there are committed and dedicated to their work, knowing their reward will be in heaven and not on earth.

We dined with one of the couples, and as they shared with us stories of God's provision to them, I couldn't help but remember Jesus' words in Matthew 6:25-34:

"Therefore I say unto you, Take no thought for your life, what ye shall eat, or what ye shall drink; nor yet for your body, what ye shall put on. Is not the life more than meat, and the body than raiment? Behold the fowls of the air: for they sow not, neither do they reap, nor gather into barns; yet your heavenly Father feedeth them. Are ye not much better than they? Which of you by taking thought can add one cubit unto his stature? And why take ye thought for raiment? Consider the lilies of the field, how they grow; they toil not, neither do they spin:

"And yet I say unto you, That even Solomon in all his glory was not arrayed like one of these. Wherefore, if God so clothe the grass of the field, which today is, and tomorrow is cast into the oven, shall He not much more clothe you, O ye of little faith? Therefore take no thought, saying, What shall we eat? or, What shall we drink? or, Wherewithal shall we be clothed? (For after all these things do the Gentiles seek:) for your heavenly Father knoweth that ye have need of all these things.

"But seek ye first the kingdom of God, and His righteousness; and all these things shall be added unto you. Take therefore no thought for the morrow: for the morrow shall take thought for the things of itself. Sufficient unto the day is the evil thereof."

✝   ✝   ✝

Our next trip took us to Papallacta, 40 miles east of Quito. Descending from the peak of a 13,000-foot mountain to the town (at the 3,000-foot level), we went from alpine to tropical conditions. The main HCJB power station is located near Papallacta. Because the road was in such bad condition, only a few of our men were allowed to visit the station. One missionary lives there, and Fred gave a good report of this facility on their return.

The final event, and the highlight of our journey, was going into the jungles of Ecuador. Thirty-two of our entourage flew there in a DC3. Fred and I were privileged to fly with Dave Gysterhaus, a Mission Aviation Fellowship pilot, in a smaller aircraft. He would swoop down, almost to the tops of the trees, to show us sights along the way. We saw dense tropical and jungle vegetation, and small huts lining both sides of the river. The pilot pointed to a small schoolhouse used to educate the Jivaro Indians, formerly a fierce head-hunting tribe.

Upon landing, we were taken to our accommodations where missionaries lived including one ten-room house built by martyred pilot, Nate Saint, many years ago. The next morning we were served a breakfast food that was new to us. The mission workers had grown tired of their usual oatmeal mush and had taken rolled oats, nuts and cinnamon and added oil and honey and baked it. It was delicious and chewy. This was an early version of granola we all know and love today. Looking back, we all wish they had taken our suggestion to patent their recipe.

We toured two mission hospitals, one named after the father

of Rev. Theodore Epp, founder of the Back to the Bible radio ministry. During this tour, we learned the Epp Hospital had an urgent need of an x-ray machine for diagnosing patients before surgery. They also needed an anesthesia machine. Up to this time, the only way to anesthetize a patient was by using an ether soaked cloth held to the patient's nose and mouth. I immediately added this need to my prayer list.

Instead of flying back to Quito, we took an all-day bus trip. The vistas and gorgeous scenery were well worth any time loss and inconvenience. Along the roadways grew wild, colorful orchid plants in great abundance. We saw women hand-washing piles of clothes near a gushing waterfall and travelers moving along the narrow road on foot, bicycle, motorbike, donkey, and all manner of rusted vehicles.

We had brought gospel literature printed in Spanish and enjoyed tossing these out of the bus windows to curious villagers as we drove by. Knowing that over a thousand villages had yet to be reached with the gospel, our prayers flew out the windows with every tract in hopes that God's Word would not return void.

Ruth and Fred cross the Equator.

The day of our departure had arrived, but on our appearance at the Quito airport, we heard an announcement over the loudspeaker that our flight had been cancelled. In fact, our plane had not even touched down but had continued on to Bogota, Colombia, because severe weather conditions had moved in.

"God always has a reason." I said to our tour group. Someone else quoted Romans 8:28, "All things work together for good to those who love God and are the called according to His purpose."

Avianca Airlines provided hotel and food expenses for us to stay the extra day in Quito. When we arrived in Miami, we learned one of our tour members led a flight attendant to Christ. Now we understood why God allowed us to stay an extra day. It was to reach this woman on her vacation. Little did she know that she was taking the weekend off to make the most important decision of her life—to receive Jesus.

Thinking over the events of our journey while flying home, I prayed, "Lord, I will do anything for the mission field." Yes, I knew I had it in my heart to show my slides in order to raise money for the down payment on that IBM typesetter machine. But, as I sat there with Fred dozing at my side, God spoke to me again to believe him to provide the X-ray machine and anesthesia machine as well!

"Wow! That's a big order!" I said to myself, careful not to disturb Fred and the other passengers. I closed my eyes and wondered how God was going to bring all this about.

We arrived home on Friday and that Sunday morning at church, a woman I knew sat in the pew behind me. She tapped me on the shoulder and whispered, "Ruth, do you know anyone who needs an X-ray machine?"

What? How amazing that she asked me of all people. I promptly said, "Yes! Yes I do!" She told me that George Junior Republic, a nearby boys' correctional school, had an X-ray machine they wanted to donate.

The next day, I called the HCJB headquarters in Florida telling them that I had an X-ray machine for them. They, of course, wanted to know if this machine was in good working condition. I told them that I would have it checked out.

When I hung up, a thought came to me. Dr. Sikorsky was the one who read X-rays at our local hospital. I went in to talk to him and told him about the X-ray machine and the need to know if it was in good condition. After hearing my concerns, Dr. Sikorsky put his hand under his chin and said, "The man you need to ask about this services the X-ray equipment in all the hospitals in this area. In fact, he'll be coming in on Friday, I'll call you when he arrives," Dr. Sikorsky said.

On Friday morning, God spoke to me to go to the hospital at 10 a.m. and not wait for the doctor to call. So, I got in my car and drove over to the hospital and parked my car in the lot at the same time another car also pulled up nearby. A man got out of his car, and I got out of mine, and we both headed towards the entrance. He and I walked through the front door at the same time. Dr. Sikorsky was there standing in the lobby as we entered. He laughed as he said, "That's him!" He pointed to the same man who had walked in with me, "That is the man you need to see." God's amazing timing!

When I told the man about the X-ray machine being discarded at George Junior Republic, he offered to go with me straightaway. After careful evaluation, he said the machine was in great condition and had hardly been used.

"It will be perfect for use on the mission field,"

"So how much do I owe you for coming to examine it?"

He smiled and said, "Nothing, this one is on me." I could hardly contain myself as I made the call that night to HCJB.

The next morning while at work, my mind could not stop

thinking of the other need I had encountered—for an anesthesia machine. I felt I was to contact Dr. Sikorsky again to seek his help. After work, I took courage and stopped to see the doctor in person at his home.

Dr. Sikorsky listened attentively to my story of the other need at Epp Mission Hospital. "Mrs. Chase, our hospital has just upgraded and purchased a new anesthesia machine, but the old one is still in great working condition. You can write a letter to the Hospital Board of Directors. They will discuss this at the next board meeting, and I am sure they will give you the machine."

A week later, when the board met together, I took a seat on the bench just outside the boardroom to pray and wait. I watched the doctors and board members go in. Thankfully, I didn't have long to wait as the decision on the anesthesia machine was the first item on the agenda.

Imagine my joy when one of the men came out, looked at me with a smile on his face and said, "Mrs. Chase, you can have the anesthesia machine, it was unanimous."

The "big order" had been filled. It was settled and decided. Soon, the equipment was packed and crated by one of our church members who just so happened to be a professional mover. He smiled at me and said, "You have done enough!" My church had taken an offering to pay for the shipping fees and soon the crates were on their way to the HCJB headquarters in Florida. The office there in turn, sent them onward to the Epp Mission Hospital in Shell, Ecuador.

God is a God of abundance. As I continued to show my slides of the work in Ecuador for three months, God generously provided $1,000—that's $250 more than the amount needed for the IBM typesetter machine.

Ephesians 3:20 says, "Now unto him that is able to do exceeding abundantly above all that we ask or think..." God is faithful!

In January 2014, HCJB Global (Heralding Christ Jesus' Blessing), changed its name to Reach Beyond, now based in Colorado Springs. I am so grateful to God for missionaries who obey the Great Commission and go into all the world to preach the gospel.

We can all have a part and respond in different ways: some will go, some will stay, some will give, and some will pray. I will forever be grateful that I was one of those God chose to use for this task.

To God be all the praise and glory!

World Gospel Mission tour to Bolivia

"Work ... while it is day; the night cometh
when no man can work" (John 9:4, KJ21).

As I continue in my Christian walk, I've found that the times
I've felt closest to God were when I traveled to different mission
fields and participated in kingdom work. I am thankful whenever and however God has used me to touch someone's life along
the way. "Great is the LORD, and greatly to be praised" (Psalm
145:3, NKJV).

One such trip was when Fred and I actually took two teenagers with us to the mission field. Both showed a love for God
and a desire to serve Him. The girl, Carol Owens, attended our
church; in fact, she was the pastor's daughter and from a good,
Christian home. The young man, David Hankin, had shared
with us his desire to be a missionary someday. Both were about
17 years old, and we began to talk to them about the possibility
of traveling with us on our next mission trip to Bolivia in South
America.

Somehow, this all came together beautifully and their parents
felt right about their going with us to Bolivia with this organization called World Gospel Mission. We prayed this would be a
good step toward their future calling. Also coming with us on
this trip was my sister Twila Hoffman.

Bolivia is located just below the equator, and our trip was to be in the month of July. I knew our summer would be their winter, so I packed expecting the weather to be just the opposite of ours. Oh yes, I prayed for the weather to be warm as I have a hard time with the cold, but I still packed for chilly weather. Well, wouldn't you know it? I was not packing in faith, the weather turned out to be hot most of the time we were there.

Bolivia's largest city, Santa Cruz, was founded in the 16th century. However, the city remained archaic in many ways. After 400 years, they were just beginning to pave their streets, placing this city as one of the most primitive and impoverished cities in South America.

Upon our arrival to Santa Cruz, we were told our hotel reservations were cancelled because a group of pilots had been flown in to do an emergency search and rescue for a downed plane. Fortunately, we were able to get accommodations at the mission station with World Gospel Mission.

In 1973, Bolivia was going through a time of political unrest with workman strikes and demonstrations which the missionaries told us were instigated for the most part by Communists. All this turmoil affected everyone, even the schools and students. It was alarming to hear that after the students had participated in demonstrations and protest gatherings, the teachers followed suit and had a strike as well. Because of all this upheaval, the public schools had been closed all year. David and Carol, the teenagers who were accompanying us, were in shock. They could not imagine anything like this taking place in America.

The local missionaries warned us we might be required to stop at various check points when we traveled on the highways. Sure enough, certain roads would be blocked off randomly at various times. This created fear, distrust, and each day the tension increased.

We had planned a journey to the mountains and nearly cancelled because most gas stations had closed due to Chaco War veterans staging strike demonstrations. The pickup truck we were to ride in was low on gas, and so it did not look good for us to go. But then the World Gospel missionaries surprised us by siphoning gasoline from two of their mission jeeps so we could make the trip.

As we traveled on the bumpy roads in the back of that pickup truck, I thought of the many times I would sit in the comfort of my living room, watching the evening news on television and hear of unrest in different parts of the world. But I know now that until you are actually there in the middle of it all, it is hard to truly understand it.

Nearly every day we were in Bolivia, we were in some church. Although we could not understand a single word of the sermons being preached, we felt united with these believers through God's Holy Spirit. We enjoyed hearing the congregations sing, and we were pleased when a familiar hymn would be sung. Then the English words in our memory bank would translate the meaning in our mind.

On our first day in the mission church in Santa Cruz, I looked up the passage of Scripture the pastor read in Isaiah 6:5: "Woe is me! for I am undone; because I am a man of unclean lips."

To prepare Isaiah for God's service, an angel of the Lord took a hot coal from the temple altar and placed it on his lips. Isaiah was now ready and prepared for God's service. Then God asked, "Whom shall I send, and who will go for Us?" and Isaiah's answer was, "Here am I! Send me" (v.8).

Jesus' last commission to His disciples was, "Go ye into all the world, and preach the gospel to every creature" (Mark 16:15).

Not everyone is called to be a foreign missionary or minister

of the gospel, but everyone is called to serve the Lord. I felt grati-
fied to be there with Fred, my sister Twila, and David and Carol
who now had this opportunity to taste missions first hand.

There are many ways to serve the Lord: For instance, it can
be singing in a church choir or teaching Sunday School, or visiting the sick and elderly, or even sending cards of greeting and
encouragement. We can all cheer others when they are in need
of a kind word, affirmation, or help of some kind. Last, but not
least, is prayer. We can and should pray for missionaries and
support them as stated in Matthew 9:37-38: "Then saith He unto
His disciples, 'The harvest truly is plenteous, but the laborers are
few; Pray ye therefore the Lord of the harvest, that He will send
forth laborers into His harvest.'"

That night 18 people went to the altar to seek God. The folks
there were not as anxious as we are to go home after the meeting.
Their services were lengthy, and the testimony meetings did not
even begin until 10:45 p.m.

The tiny mission outposts in the jungle were too small to
accommodate our entire group of sixteen, so we were divided
into four groups of four people each: Fred and I and two others,
a man and woman, formed one group; my sister Twila, and the
two young people we brought with us, went on another team.

Our foursome, were asked to go to a Christian Mission School
Farm. It was there, we met a couple in their fifties who used to
run a farm in the states. Now, they directed the operating of this
Bolivian farm with the help of four other teachers. Together,
they oversaw the education of 85 children. About half of these
students resided on the farm while the rest commuted to the
premises each day. At noon every day, a hearty lunch would be
served up to the entire student body, utilizing the fresh farm pro-
duce. Through the media of education, these children now had

an opportunity to hear the gospel message and receive a quality education.

During our time there, the students put on a wonderful musical performance for us. We needed no interpreter to translate the excellence of their talent and music abilities. We were delighted to hear that all but two of the children had received Christ as their Savior.

This couple was doing an amazing job with the children, and we discovered they were also reaching out to many adults as well. Every week, for miles around, villagers would come to the farm to receive emergency dental care. The husband would do extractions and teach hygiene while his wife had learned to make false teeth and even partial plates for those in need. I am not sure where they learned these skills, but I am certain that these gifts were well received in this country. Along with dental care, people heard the gospel message, and many were finding Christ through this ministry. In just the last month before our arrival, we heard that almost one hundred came to Christ at the dental clinic.

While at the farm one day, I noticed a young native Indian girl pounding out the rice from the chaff. She would then take a bowl and pour it from one bowl to the other causing all the chaff to be carried away in the wind. As I sat there watching this novel scene, it brought to my mind the Scripture in Psalm 1:4 that says, "The ungodly are ... like the chaff which the wind drives away" (NKJV).

That afternoon, we all had a fun opportunity to ride on horseback. I had never done this before, and so Jim Benson, one of our group, invited me to ride with him on his horse. It was a little frightening at first, but soon I relaxed and started to enjoy the experience as we galloped along. Suddenly, the horse made an abrupt halt and both Jim and I landed on the cold, hard ground.

Apparently, this labeled us as the "entertainment committee" for the day and sure enough, we looked up to find everyone else laughing at us as we stood and brushed the grass and dirt off our clothing. Someone jokingly shouted out, "Look at that, he's just like a sinner. He never goes down alone, but takes someone else with him!" Well, I was just thankful that neither of us got hurt.

Later that day, the pilot at whose home we were to spend the night arrived at the farm with another group. The flight to this station was only 15 minutes by air, but had we traveled on horseback, it would have taken nine hours. These are the only modes of transport to this mission station other than hiking in for days. We heard that Bolivia is the highest and most isolated country in South America, and we were beginning to believe it.

The new group stayed there at the farm school, and our foursome flew on to another jungle mission station. Fortunately, this one had roads; but sad to say, the roads were in such poor condition that it took our jeep one hour to drive a mere 12 miles. While we were there, we were introduced to the local Christians, visited their churches, and prayed for their success.

One night, we returned to the mission station rather late having attended an evening church meeting. In order to get back to our housing, we had to cross a river, but the barge attendant had gone to bed thinking no one would be crossing that night because of the lateness of the hour and because it was beginning to drizzle.

As always, we prayed while our missionary guide went looking for the barge pilot. It was dark and wet outside, and we began to think we would have to spend the night sleeping in the jeep. Our missionary friend had warned us that he had to sleep in his vehicle on quite a few occasions.

Before too long he returned to us having located the barge pilot who said he would take us over the river but he would have to raise the fare to include an extra $6.20 above the regular fare. We knew he wanted to take advantage of the situation and make a little more money but, we felt it was well worth it not having to bunk in a crowded vehicle.

We were glad the weather was not too cold that night, but across the river, we found the clay roads were wet and slippery. At times it looked like we could slip right off the road at any moment.

It was nearly midnight when we arrived back to the base. I promised myself that I would never again take for granted the comforts back home without remembering to pray for our hard-working, self-sacrificing missionaries and the difficult challenges they faced day after day to bring God's Word to the lost. The missionaries in Bolivia lived simply with homes that had dirt floors, no electricity, no hot water, and no indoor toilets. A simple shower facility was made by using a large, galvanized metal drum to hold water. At the bottom a hose and faucet were connected to a shower head that could be turned off and on.

When the day arrived for us to begin our homeward journey, we had planned to leave at 3:30 in the afternoon. However, but the missionaries moved up the departure time to 10:30 a.m. It would take us at least an hour and a half to drive to the river. We were to discover that this change was God's intervention for us all.

The missionaries had been on radio communication, and they had notified each other that this day was an especially harrowing one. Extreme caution was the alert given. By our leaving sooner, they hoped to help us by pass any troublesome check-points. We sensed the concern on the missionaries' faces. We knew the Communist rebels were behind this.

As we arrived at our check station, a soft rain started to fall. The missionary who drove us there had his two small children with him. He told us that he would walk us to the river as he was not allowed to drive past the checkpoint. This would mean he would have to leave his two children asleep in the back of the jeep during this time.

"We won't hear of you doing this," we told him. "No, you can-not leave those two babies to come help us. We are adults, we can make it on our own." We had been aware of a growing anger building up in the Communists at the checkpoint, and it would not be right to put the children in further danger.

After we left him, the missionary, still concerned for our well-being, was able to find a man with a motorcycle who caught up with us and offered us rides at least part of the way. Only two of us could fit on his bike at a time while he rode sitting on the gas tank. Even with this assist, it was slow going as he drove back and forth to transport us. The road had deep ruts and cracks and the bike would slip at times. When needed, we got off the bike and walked on the wet muddy road. Bit by bit, we reached our destination on time.

No one was there at the barge pick up, not even the barge pilot, so we decided it would be best to find shelter and wait as the drizzle was getting heavier. Part of all the commotion at the checkpoints were from people protesting the work being done to build the bridge. The local people felt the work just wasn't getting done fast enough. Then too, the Communists had got-ten involved to create even more agitation. We found that if we stood under some of the already erected supports of the bridge, we could stay dry, so this is what we did.

We waited there for over an hour until finally, the man with the motorcycle drove back up to where we were. He had some distressing news. It appeared that the four-member group and missionary that was to have met us at the barge, had been detained at another checkpoint. They were not allowed to continue on foot as we had. This was serious.

The man with the motor bike told us we could go back to the missionaries' home and he would help us get back, but he also said that we could decide to go ahead and board the barge and cross the river in hopes of meeting the other two teams on the other side. The rain had lifted, and we needed to make this important decision.

Should we go back, or cross the river hoping to reunite with the other two groups?

As we prayed, we had a sense of God's presence all around us. We had peace in our hearts that we were to go forward and not turn back. Any fear we had in our hearts was gone. We thanked the man on the motorcycle, and the four of us boarded the old barge that carried us across the river. Once on the other side, we began to realize that because the other two groups were not there and it was past the time of our rendezvous, that they may have been detained as well.

We had no idea where we were! We decided to walk until we could find the main road and perhaps locate a bus to drive us the 80 miles to Santa Cruz. We were thankful we were not carrying heavy luggage. There were no houses in sight and not a person to be seen anywhere. Even if we had met someone, how could we communicate our need?

After walking a bit, we came to a fork in the road. "Now,

what?" Fred asked. "Which road should we take?" It was frightening to think we could easily take a wrong turn. We needed to be in Santa Cruz today as our flight home would leave tomorrow morning. We hesitated there for about ten minutes in prayer when all of a sudden he said, "Look, there's a jeep coming in our direction!" Sure enough, one was headed our way. "Perhaps we can stop it and pay the driver to take us to Santa Cruz!" I said.

As the jeep got closer to us, we were joyously surprised to find the driver was the missionary we had been waiting for! He had with him in the jeep, one of the other groups and in that group was my sister, Twila. She seemed very relieved to see us.

We had no choice but to all load up into that jeep. Somehow, we were able to squeeze in tightly. The ride on the way to Santa Cruz was loud and animated as we each shared adventure stories of our time in the jungle villages. Twila told me that she had slept in a house filled with bats that kept her awake all night. Thankfully, we had no further delays or checkpoints as we bounced along towards the city. We arrived in Santa Cruz safe and sound about 4:00 p.m.

We anxiously awaited news of the other two teams not with us. They had not been allowed to go past the checkpoints, and so the mission decided to airlift them out of their dangerous locations.

So, two groups made it out and two had to be flown in to the city. That night we were all together again. We had plenty to talk over as we sat down and enjoyed a hearty dinner together.

Our two teenagers looked none the worse for wear. They did not complain about anything they endured, and Fred and I were careful not to leave them with any negative images. Fred whispered to me, "Do you think David will want to be a missionary after all this?"

"Well, they certainly have had a good test to prepare them for what the mission field can be like," I said. We were glad David and Carol had survived and even said they were glad they had come on this journey with us.

After dinner, we paused to thank God for His watchful care over us. We prayed for the protection of the missionaries in their homes in the jungle. We had all participated in a blessed and meaningful experience together. We decided it might be best to turn in for the night instead of attending the evening church service. The moment my head hit the pillow, I was fast asleep.

Next morning, before heading to the airport, we were given the news that two of the missionary families and their children, ten people in all, had been placed under house arrest. We realized that all of us escaped the jungle at just the right time. Had we delayed, we too, would have been placed under house arrest with great uncertainty about our future. We certainly would have missed our flight home, and it would be hard to say how long we would be detained in Bolivia. Psalm 34:7 says, "The angel of the LORD encamps around those who fear Him, and delivers them" (NKJV).

The newspapers reported that the Communist soldiers had taken 26 North American hostages including some of the missionaries we stayed with. Our prayers had new meaning as we prayed for Bolivia and its leadership. They had gone through four presidents in the past two years, and we did our best to keep informed of their political progress. After our return to the states, we were thrilled to hear that the takeover had failed, and the newest government was turning away from Communism and moving forward. God still rules and overrides man's plans.

The Bolivian people are very open to the gospel message and the changes in government are making it easier for the spread and growth of Christianity. Missionaries working there need our continual prayer and financial support

As for our two teens, Carol went to college and met and married a pastor, and they serve together today in church ministry.

David also married, had children and he and his wife took the leap to be missionaries in Burkina Faso in Africa. We knew he had a call of God on his life and helped him with tuition to train for his mission career. When we read of the work he was doing and the poverty conditions where he was serving -- some were dying of starvation -- Fred and I were prompted by the Lord to send financial offerings to purchase food to feed the hungry.

David and his family would still be in Africa today had they not been involved in a head-on collision in that country. I saw photos of their wrecked vehicle, and everyone told us that their survival was a miracle as all the family members walked away from the totaled truck. They all recovered completely from their injuries except for David's wife who suffered the most harm. This resulted in the family leaving the mission field and returning stateside for her treatment and recuperation.

The Bible says, "Where there is no vision, the people perish" (Proverbs 29:18). This means we need to have a vision and keep it. John 9:4 is a message to us today. "Work...while it is day; the night cometh when no man can work" (KJ21).

One can never tell when the doors to a nation will close, and that is why it is so important to walk through the open doors and be faithful in spreading the gospel to all who will listen.

New hope for Finland

Of all the countries I've visited, the small Baltic nation of Finland is the one God has put on my heart most often. Between 1983 and 1988 I traveled there four times with groups from World Missionary Service and Evangelism. Our assignment was to help rebuild His church there. We would be repairing and repainting once-abandoned church buildings that Finnish pastors were seeking to fill again with worshippers.

I knew this was just a small picture of what God wanted to do in the nation. The people of Finland had struggled to survive against a harsh climate and the aggressions of its powerful neighbor, the Soviet Union. Over the centuries its church had grown almost as cold as the climate. I wanted to be part of God's work of renewal. My husband Fred was working and couldn't join us but he released me to serve as God led me.

Trusting in God's timing

My first trip to Finland didn't go as expected, but it certainly went according to God's timetable. I arrived at Pittsburgh's airport on the afternoon of August 12, 1983, and was told my connecting flight to New York would be 45 minutes late. It turned out to be two hours late. Realizing I was going to miss my plane in New York, I asked a flight attendant to call Fred Reitz, our World Missionary Service and Evangelism tour director, and ask him to leave my passport at the Finnair desk.

I wasn't worried. I had so often seen the Lord use changing circumstances as opportunities. When a young couple asked what I would do about missing my flight with the group, I assured them God had my circumstances under control. "It says in Romans 8:28, 'We know that all things work together for good to them that love God, to them who are the called according to His purpose.' He called me on this trip.

"I feel bad for the group," I said, "and especially the tour director, but not for myself. I've had perfect peace." Then I quoted Isaiah 26:3: "Thou wilt keep him in perfect peace, whose mind is stayed on thee: because he trusteth in Thee."

I knew I was in the center of God's will, God had chosen me to go to Finland. The previous fall I read in *The Explorer* about the trip. I wrote asking if I could go. The reply was, "We're only taking two single women, and those places have been filled." I accepted this but prayed, *God if you want me to go, make an opening.* In January one of the women cancelled, and I replaced her.

I arrived in New York at the Finnair office only to find them

My new friends from Iran – Susan and Gimmy

closed, but there was a telephone number to call. Thank God they had my passport upstairs in the office. They gave me two tickets, one flying Lufthansa to Frankfurt, Germany, then changing planes and flying Finnair to Helsinki. Several times they reminded me that I would be flying standby.

I took a taxi to the Lufthansa gate, since by then there was only one hour until flight time. I arrived to find at least 15 persons on stand-by. The computer came up with my name four times before finally it confirmed that I was able to board the plane. No accidents with God.

The Lord placed me beside Susan, a young woman from Iran who was flying with her 8-year-old daughter, Gimmy. Susan was very upset that they also had missed their scheduled flight. I explained that I had missed my plane and my group was to arrive in Helsinki five hours before me and go on without me.

"I'm not concerned because God is in control," I said.

"You are a comfort," she replied.

"I'm a Christian, and the Lord has promised to take care of His people. He said to cast our cares on Him, and that's what I'm doing."

"I've known many people who said they were Christians but you are different. Frankly, I've lost faith in all religions."

"What's a Christian?" Gimmy asked.

Her mother smiled at me. I turned to Gimmy and told her as simply as I could about Jesus and the plan of salvation. I then gave Susan the book *What the Bible is All About* and some other Christian literature.

It's so exciting to serve Jesus. He is continually providing opportunities for His people to share their faith. I believe that God rerouted me for just that purpose. I don't know whatever happened with that young mother and child. As 1 Corinthians

3:6 says, I planted the seed, someone else will water it and God will give the increase. I believe I will see them in heaven. We serve a great, big and wonderful God!

Ella Hellsten, wife of the Methodist Church pastor in Helsinki, came to the airport for me. I stayed in their home that night. The city was rocking with activity. The first-ever World Championships of the International Association of Athletics Federations (IAAF) were underway, attracting athletes from 159 countries. Some of our group attended the Hellstens' church that Sunday. When my luggage finally arrived, I was taken to Inga and united with the rest of the group. There were 23 of us from eight states.

Inga is a village a few miles up the Baltic coast from Helsinki. At the evening meeting there, Rev. Erik Hellsten told us we were an answer to prayer. "A year and a half ago some of us decided to reopen this church, which had been closed for 20 years. It was in such bad repair we became discouraged. Then we learned that some Americans were willing to come and help restore it. What a joy!"

Pastor Hellsten and his family

Our group stayed in some rooms at a nearby Agricultural School, doing our own cooking.

I led one of our first devotions, teaching from Nehemiah chapters 1–6 about rebuilding the walls of Jerusalem. Nehemiah was a man of prayer, action, courage, and perseverance. He prayed before his action, during his action and after his action. The people had a mind to work (4:6), and the walls were finished in 52 days (6:15). I could not have imagined how appropriate that Word would be for our team.

Monday we arrived at the church and found all the pews piled up and the floors dug up. I wish I had a picture of our faces as we viewed the project. The walls needed to be brushed down, patched and mesh-glued on the patched area. Two coats of white paint on the ceiling, sandalwood on the walls. The pews had to be washed with a strong solution, sanded, painted one coat of white and two coats of brown. The woodwork had to be scraped. They burned the paint off some doors. We had to scrape 103 windows, undercoat them and put on the finishing coat. We completed 41 windows. Our efforts were reported on the front page in the local newspaper.

I love to walk, and most days several of us walked the two miles to and from the church.

I prayed for the nation as I walked, and it made me feel at home there. As I walked past fields ready for harvest, it reminded me of John 4:35: "... Lift up your eyes and look on the fields; for they are white already to harvest." And in Matthew 9:38, Jesus reminds us of our need to pray that God will send more harvesters because they are few. So in faith I ask, "Send more to Finland, Lord!"

Before coming home we took a short trip to Leningrad by a Russian train. The moment we crossed the border we felt the oppressive spirit there as guards confiscated our magazines and newspapers. Leningrad, now called by its original name St. Petersburg, was the summer home of Russia's czars. The city is full of palaces, and Peter the Great's palace is now a spectacular museum called The Hermitage.

Saturday evening we went to a Baptist church in Leningrad. They claim membership of 3,000, and I could sense true spiritual hunger in the city. During the two-hour service, three different people preached short sermons. I saw tears in the eyes of many worshippers as the choir sang traditional hymns in Russian. At one point, a child was dedicated to God. Only the grandmother was a Christian. The congregation cried as the grandmother and pastor prayed. They asked all to pray for the family.

Many of us prayed for more religious freedom in Russia, and in a few years God would answer that prayer with the crumbling of the Soviet Union. Our team spent just two weeks in Finland. We accomplished much, but there was considerably more left to do. We prayed that God would inspire others to finish the work at the church so it would be reopened to His glory.

Finishing the task

A year later God opened the way for me to return to Finland to continue to work on the churches. Fred Reitz led our team again, and five of the ten people in our group had been on the tour the year before. After a seven-hour flight from New York, the Hellstens met us in Helsinki and drove us out to Inga. Once again we stayed at the school and got into much the same routine as we had before. Midway through our trip, we finished the work in Inga. We were privileged to attend the first service there.

Later we boarded the *Viking Song* for the 14-hour trip to Stockholm, Sweden. From our hotel we ventured out to see Stockholm's Royal Palace, took a boat ride under the city's four-teen bridges, and went up the Kaknäs Tower for a sweeping view of the area.

Upon our return to Helsinki, the group went by train to

After 20 years, what joy to see the pews filled again!

Hango, site of our second work project. We stayed at a Lutheran school and walked each day to the Hango United Methodist Church to scrape, repair and paint the outside. I climbed a scaffold to paint the eaves of the church as there was no one else to do so. I'd never done anything like that, and it was a miracle I was able to do it without fear.

After three days of dedicated scraping and painting, the old church was looking brighter. At the end of our time there the precious ladies of the church presented our group with a beautiful rug. Klaus, the pastor of the church, read us a farewell note. Our eyes filled with tears. I thought it would be nice to have the note, but I didn't ask anyone, including God. Yet at the end of the service, the note was given to *me*. Once again God gave me my heart's desire; I still have the original which was written in Swedish. Here is what it said in English:

Farewell to our friends from a far distant land. We have been bound together with everlasting ties. At the Holy Supper we experienced it most. It was like a breath of the Spirit from the Lord.

Unselfish offer work and job. We saw your spirit and were silent. We cannot understand nor can we gather that people can work out of themselves, but merely by the love of God.

We want to say thanks and want to get pen pals but language barrier forbids us to do so. We want to say thank you in this way, and the rest you will get as a heavenly reward.

Thank you for warmth and sunshine you gave us. We keep it until we meet again in heaven at last. Every evening star is shining over days past. Every morning God walks over the country and wakes us up to do His will.

The ladies gave each of us a rose. We accomplished much at Hango. We got almost three sides painted. We trusted God would send others to finish the project.

Land of the Midnight Sun

In July of 1986 I was off to Finland again. Our group of ten assembled at the Finnair counter in New York's Kennedy International Airport, and I knew all but four of them. I told the group I lived near Grove City, Pennsylvania. One of the women, Janica Mitchell, said her sister lived there. Well, it happened to be Nancy Humble who I have known for a long time. It's a small, small world after all.

We arrived in Helsinki, and once again the Hellstens met us at the airport. This time our assignment was in Kristinestad, a six-hour bus trip. The pastor, Tom Norstrom, greeted us. We were taken to the church, where we reviewed our work project: painting the outside of an historic Swedish Methodist Church. Another tough job!

Most of us had jet lag, but we scraped and painted with little sleep. I felt God's presence as I recalled Psalm 29:11, "The Lord will give strength to His people" (NKJV). I knew people back home were praying. The power of prayer reaches across oceans!

The next week our team flew to Rovaniemi above the Arctic Circle. Here in the land of the midnight sun, they have 24 hours of daylight May through July. One day the tour went north to go white-water rafting down the rapids, which was the highlight of the trip to Lapland. I asked our boat trip guide (above) about the winter, when this area gets two months of darkness. He said it's mostly dark but whatever light they have reflects off the white snow, allowing them to ski four to five hours a day.

Our group stayed in beautiful log cabins with saunas. One evening we gathered at Jan's cabin and watched a 15-minute local television news clip about our group. I joked that we had to go all the way to Lapland to be on TV. We hated to leave our beautiful log cabins, but knew our duty was to go back to work. On the ride to the airport I saw a reindeer and her fawn. Beautiful!

We went to the church for dinner on the day we arrived back, but Pastor Tom forgot to order our dinner. So we walked over to a new restaurant in town. Tom came to the restaurant red-faced.

"Don't worry. You're entitled to one mistake," I said.

"Well, this was my first mistake," he laughed.

"To make up for it you should have to cook our dinner," someone quipped.

"That would be a second mistake."

Now everyone was laughing.

LAND OF THE MIDNIGHT SUN
Our group stayed in beautiful log cabins, complete with saunas.
It was 3 a.m. when I snapped this photo in Lapland.

Ruth and members of the team painting the church in Kristinestad, Finland.

The next three days we scraped and painted all day. The TV station came back to make a half-hour program about these Americans who came all the way to Finland to paint their city's historic Methodist Church. Every newspaper in the country had reported about us too. Saturday evening we went to the Congregational Church, which hadn't had a service for three years. A new believer named Beris Lindholm led the service. He sang for us with a soaring voice that touched us all. Tears came to his eyes as he worshipped. You could see in his face how much he loved the Lord. Beris invited us to his new home for coffee time and a prayer of dedication. What a blessed time! As Jesus said in Matthew 18:20, "For where two or three are gathered together in My name, there am I in the midst of them."

We painted the church most of a second coat of paint. Church leaders bought new storm windows, but because of its age the historical society made them paint the old ones.

The church threw a going-away party to express their appreciation for our work. They presented each of us with a book about Kristinestad, signed by the author. It was hard to say goodbye as we left on our six-hour bus ride to Helsinki. Once again I thanked God for the beautiful weather which enabled us to do more outside painting than expected. Much was accomplished for God's glory. My great hope was that soon those churches would be full!

The fourth painting venture

My last journey to Finland with World Missionary Service and Evangelism brought together a group of 16 people from seven states. It began on July 25, 1988, and we were once more welcomed in Helsinki by Ella and Erik Hellsten. They put us on a bus to Kristinestad, and there to greet us were the familiar faces of Pastor Tim and Hilde Norstrom, Helga Heinkila, and Mrs. Bror Grankvill. Our assignment this time was the sanctuary of the church, which had not been painted for 50 years!

Our dorm was in a nursery school about two miles from the church. I walked every morning to the church and back in the evening. At night we had team meetings. After one, some of us women were discussing "heater points" of the body. The tour director heard the word heater, and he shut the door. His wife said he sometimes only hears a word or two, and he assumes the rest. He thought we were cold. At times, I think we all are guilty of assumption, which can be sin. This reminded me of times God had spoken to me about misjudging something because I didn't have all the facts.

The following Monday we painted all day. The local TV station came to film another half-hour program. The story of Americans painting the sanctuary of the Swedish-speaking Methodist Church would be aired in the fall. We also made the front page of the newspaper again. That evening, Marilyn, Erik, Cindy and I were invited to the home of TV producer Olle Haavisto to view the video of the group two years ago, and also the one taken that day. I was impressed with the half-hour program he made from the interviews and the church group singing.

Anne, his daughter, is a gifted ceramic artist and gave Cindy one of her painted tiles. Right away I wanted a special plate painted by Anne. It felt like a selfish wish, but then I thought of Psalm 37:4-5, "Delight thyself also in the LORD: and He shall give thee the desires of thine heart. Commit thy way unto the LORD; trust also in Him; and He shall bring it to pass."

Just like the "thank you note" God gave me, He blessed me without my giving voice to my desire. I received one of Anne's plates in the mail after I arrived home. The plate depicts a girl who stopped walking along so she could watch a squirrel. It reads, "Taking a moment to take it easy is being a friend to yourself." I think that's good advice. The back reads, "There's a star in the sky called The Star of Love –I'm looking for it, and I believe I'll find it." Love, Anne Haavisto 1989." That star she's looking for is the Morning Star, Jesus.

In two days our energetic group managed to complete two coats of paint on most of the sanctuary. It looked stunning! The church family was so grateful, and it seemed to bring new energy to the whole congregation. None of us in the group were professional painters, but God had put it on our hearts to serve the church of Finland. We did that with all our hearts.

The last part of our journey included a 50-mile ferry trip across the Gulf of Finland to Tallinn, Estonia. The small Baltic country was then still under the rule of the Soviet Union (USSR). We visited Pastor Olay Pammets and had great fellowship with his wife, son and three daughters who entertained us by singing and playing the piano. Pastor Pammets shared his dream that someday their Methodist congregation would have their own church building. He said for 38 years they have worshiped in the

Seventh Day Adventist Church's building.

Their own church building burned down decades ago, and they worshiped in a small chapel until the Russians took over the building for a radio station. Under Communist rule, the state tells the church where they can worship. Estonia has its own rich history, but until the USSR crumbled in late 1989, the capital was overshadowed by monuments to Stalin and Lenin.

On Sunday we went to the Methodist service, and what a joy to see it was standing room only. Our group sang and there was three sermons, one by a guest speaker from Ashbury College in Kentucky. That night we returned to Helsinki, praising God for the faith of those precious Estonian believers. I can still see their faces, their longing for freedom. Although the country is independent now, and there's more individual freedom, the church is still struggling.

My four trips to Finland and the outings to nearby countries left me with a great love and respect for the believers there. I'm forever grateful for their kindness and hospitality—and for their commitment to keep serving the Lord in difficult circumstances.

The Southwest Indian School

Delight thyself also in the LORD: *and He shall give thee the desires of thine heart. Commit thy way unto the* LORD; *trust also in Him; and He shall bring it to pass (Psalm 37:4-5).*

For years Fred and I received pamphlets from the World Missionary Service and Evangelism Organization which led tours of mission work around the world. One pamphlet focused on the Southwest Indian School in Arizona. I read about the school, viewed photos of the children, prayed for them, and began to nurture a desire to go there. I wanted to help in the work and see those Native American children for myself. I discovered they had a volunteer program that gave people like me an opportunity to serve there, so that's what I decided to do.

I called the tour director, Fred Reitz, to see if they had room for one more person. He told me that all the spots had been filled. Of course, this was not the news I wanted to hear, but I figured the Lord just didn't want me to go at this time, and I accepted His will.

As the departure date grew closer, the desire to be part of that group was still stirring in my heart. I remember telling God, "Lord, please don't let me feel this way!"

On Friday, I thought to myself, *I'll try calling just one more time.* I then began to procrastinate, thinking, *Maybe I'll just call on Monday morning instead.* All that weekend, I couldn't help feeling that perhaps I should have called on Friday.

Monday morning arrived, and I called Fred Reitz once again. He said, "Mrs. Chase, I have good news and some bad news too. The good news is that someone has cancelled, and there is now room for you on the tour. The bad news is that had you called last week, we could have gotten you to Arizona at the cheaper airfare. You needed to get your ticket two weeks in advance for the best rate, now the fare has gone up $200 more."

I should have realized sooner that God was trying to get my attention, and now I had to learn my lesson the hard way. Obey God or suffer the consequences. But God is kind and good, and He was giving me my heart's desire. I packed my bags and went, rejoicing to serve the Lord at the Southwest Indian School.

There were many service opportunities at the school. Plenty involved working indoors, but the spring weather was pleasant, so I chose a job that would let me work outdoors.

I noticed a project was under way to build a shower facility.

Ruth helps with a building project at the Southwest Indian School.

When I asked if I could help with the project, they hesitatingly gave me permission, as it involved carrying heavy cement blocks to the masons who would then fit them in place to build the walls.

The Native American children who attended the school came to where I was working and asked me, "Mrs. Chase, why are you doing such hard work?" I answered, "It was my choice. This is what I wanted to do here." I think it was hard for them to understand why a woman would want to do a hard labor job usually done by men.

One of the perks of working outside was getting to know some of the native children. One day I learned of a young boy who was enrolled in the school but his parents were poor and did not have the funds to pay the remainder of his tuition. Wanting to help him out, I secretly paid the amount he owed. I was told later that he kept asking the school office, "Someone paid my bill? Who paid my bill?" Finally, they told him I was the one. He was profoundly grateful. I soon learned that he was a talented artist, and the school directors told me he was particularly gifted in pencil drawings.

One day he surprised me by giving me a drawing he had made. It still hangs proudly in my dining room at home. Not long after, in gratitude for my financial giving through the years, the school gave me another of his works. I so enjoyed these children and admired the work this school was accomplishing in these precious lives.

I remember the night our tour group overheard the children as they watched a movie together. We were told they were seeing a Western about a battle between white soldiers and Indians. I never knew the name of the movie, but we certainly could tell who they were cheering for. When the Indians were winning the battle, there was such hooting and hollering. They truly sounded like a wild tribe at a pow-wow!

The second trip I made to the school in Arizona is also a joyful memory. On the day of my arrival, some of the children ran up to greet me. They remembered me and seemed genuinely happy to see me and include me in their activities. They said, "Mrs. Chase, Mrs. Chase, please come with us to the roller rink. All of us are going, and we will have the whole roller rink to ourselves. Please come!"

Well, what could I say? I wondered if I could still roller skate. At the rink I found a nice pair of tan rollers my size and sat down to lace them up. *When was the last time I actually skated?* I asked myself. *High school! Will I even remember how to skate?* I wondered. I timidly made my way out to the rink and began to skate.

As I felt those wheels rolling under my feet, heard the music playing, it all started to come back to me naturally as what to do. Suddenly, I felt like I had been transported back in time, feeling like the teenage girl back home. I remembered how much I loved wearing those special shoes that rolled me across the floor. What fun times we had then, and what a wonderful time I was having now!

I appreciated the children who were kind and stayed close to me as I skated. And I did *not* fall.

No, not once!

Abroad with God

God enabled Fred and me to travel overseas several times. It was a blessing for us to serve at mission bases, tour the Holy Land, and experience countries so different from our own. In all I've visited almost 30 countries, bringing the good news of Jesus wherever I went. I've found that living the Golden Rule (do unto others as you would have them do unto you) is a good rule for travel. Travel can be exciting, but it can also be dangerous. Whenever we were in difficult circumstances, we prayed and He helped us. Here are a few God stories from our journeys:

MONACO: We arrived in Monaco after a long flight on an overcrowded plane. Many of the passengers complained, and one woman seemed particularly upset. She said, "I am going to get another flight home."

I said, "Don't! It's going to be better going home." I didn't know that from anything I'd heard from the airline. I just sensed it by the Holy Spirit. We enjoyed our time in the tiny Mediterranean country and also visited Italy and Germany. When the day came to go home, the airline announced that we would be staying in Monaco another day—all expenses paid—as our plane had arrived, but the crew needed to rest before they could fly again. We flew home the next day in a much larger Boeing 747, and no one was crowded. In fact, many had empty seats next to them.

Surely, God had put those words in my mouth, "It's going to be better going home." I recall other times this has happened. What an awesome God!

SPAIN: Traveling with our dear friends Lloyd and Louise Kern in Madrid, we set out on a walk one afternoon to a large park and took many paths in and around the park. When it came time to return, we didn't know what path to take back to the city. We asked a lot of people, but none spoke English. Even the police couldn't help us.

So we stopped and prayed, asking God what path we should take. Thank God we found our way back to the hotel. This taught me a lesson. The Lord had helped us out of trouble, but when in a foreign country, we shouldn't always depend on others to speak our language. Come armed with a good map and other necessary travel information.

MARTINQUE: We went to this Caribbean island to visit missionaries. Upon arrival I acquired a lot of French gospel tracts. Fred wouldn't go to the beach because he heard the women there were topless. I went on anyway. I sat there with the tracts but didn't have enough nerve to pass them out. Finally, I asked God to solve the problem. All at once it started to rain. Everyone ran for shelter with heads down. I handed out all the tracts before the sun came out again. God is good!

JAMAICA: This country has beautiful waterfalls and beaches, but like all countries it has a darker side. We heeded the warnings of our guides to be careful as we traveled and rarely had difficulties. We took an old train from Montego Bay to Kingston, and arriving at the train station, some young men grabbed our suitcases out of the train window and took off. We ran to catch up with them. They didn't seem intent on theft. They took the luggage so we would pay a "porter fee." On other trips, fellow travelers have had things stolen. I don't presume on God's protection, but I do pray for it.

AUSTRIA: We went to Salzburg by bus and were delighted to see the gazebo that was in the movie *Sound of Music*. I had heard so much about the city's white Lipizzaner horses. My heart's desire was to see them. I asked God to make it possible for me to go to the Lipizzaner stable, and He did. I was surprised to see a small newborn that was all black, a little larger colt that was black and white, and one large one that was all white. I learned the breed I saw was born black and turned white. Another of the wonders of God!

It would take another book to describe all the places I've been and the wonderful people I've met. Here's a list of the other countries visited:

CUBA	PUERTO RICO
RUSSIA	BARBADOS
VIRGIN ISLANDS	CANADA
ESTONIA	SWITZERLAND
ENGLAND	GERMANY
FRANCE	LUXEMBURG
TURKEY	GREECE
EGYPT	FINLAND
JORDAN	SWEDEN
COLOMBIA	THE BAHAMAS
PERU	THE NETHERLANDS

Lessons Learned

Praying about everything

One thing I have learned in my walk with God is to pray about everything, no matter how small or big it may seem. Our concerns are His concerns.

Seek and ye shall find – Years ago, Fred and I bought a church bond and every six months we would take a coupon to the bank to receive the interest. We kept the bond in a safe at Fred's parents' home. One day Fred mentioned he was concerned about the bond because he couldn't find it in the safe. Fred spent hours searching for it because anyone could take the bond and coupons to the bank and cash them in. I was working five days a week at the time and had no extra time to be hunting things, so I got on my knees.

I asked God to help us find the bond. Fred said, "Let's go to Dad's home and look once again in the safe." I walked outside and got into the pickup, which was in the garage. My eyes suddenly fixed on Fred's workbench. At the top, I saw a brown envelope.

"Fred, what's in that envelope?"

He looked up, and his jaw dropped. "That's it!"

He then remembered he was intending to take it to the safe on the way to work. He stopped in the garage first and noticed he was running late. So he put the envelope up there and rushed off to work. After a few days he completely forgot it. Who would think to look for it in the garage up on the high ledge? Nobody but God.

One night when I put on my PJ's, a little pearl-like button was missing. I looked around but couldn't find it. When I said my prayers I told God I would like that little top button. That night I felt my hand being pried open and something deposited in it. I put it on the night stand. Awakening in the morning, I thought, *what a dream!* But there on the night stand was that button. I still remember and am in awe.

Angels to the rescue? – One eventful day I went shopping in Franklin with my neighbor Kristine. Fred had asked me to pick up a part at the auto store just outside town. So I asked Kristine if she would stop on the way because it would be closed when we returned. We were chatting, and we passed the store. She stopped and tried to turn around by backing into a dirt driveway. There was a ditch alongside it, and as she backed up, the car slid into it.

An old man sitting on his porch yelled, "You're stuck, you're stuck, you're stuck."

I prayed, "God please help as this is my fault."

Within minutes, a car stopped and four young men got out. They were all dressed up in black pants and white shirts. Without a word they picked up the back end of the car and put it on the dirt driveway. Just as quickly they were gone. That was 30 or 40 years ago but I will never forget them. I have always wondered if they were angels.

God the real estate broker – Starting in 1992, Fred and I began volunteering every winter at YWAM's University of the Nations campus in Kona, Hawaii. In 1997 we decided to buy a condo so we could extend our time in serving the Lord there.

We had been renting a place at the Kona Pacific, just across the street from the campus. We heard there were 33 Kona

Pacific units for sale for $139,000 and all needed remodeling. We prayed God would provide us one for $100,000. One man in Georgia offered his condo for sale at $108,000, and Fred suggested we purchase it. That wasn't answering my specific prayer but I agreed it was a good price. We sent him the money.

A few weeks later, the realtor Sam Moore sent us a printout listing the condos that were still for sale. Guess what! One we had looked at (and I liked) was now listed at $97,500. I pointed this out to Fred, and he said, "Buy it, and we will live in the other one until we remodel this one." I called Mr. Moore, and he said that listing might be a mistake as he didn't think any were that cheap.

However, he agreed to check and call me back. Fred and I prayed to ask what God wanted us to pay. God said $92,000. Mr. Moore called back and confirmed the $97,500 asking price. I told him to put our bid in for $89,000.

"Well, you know the owner just lowered it, so I think that was probably his rock bottom."

He submitted our offer anyway and called back to say the owner's counter offer was $92,000. So we purchased it. We remodeled it, bought furniture, new drapes, new washer and new refrigerator and with everything added in the price was $100,000. I had asked for a condo for $100,000, expecting to spend another $10,000 for remodeling and furniture. God gave us a fully remodeled and furnished place for $100,000. As Ephesians 3:20 says, He "is able to do exceedingly abundantly above all that we ask or think." What an awesome God!

I even pray about seemingly small decisions. Once I needed some large storage tubs. A friend said she had some for $20 each, but she had only one and that wasn't suitable. So I stopped by the Buyer's Fair store in Franklin, which had advertised a sale on large tubs. They had sold them all, even the floor models. The clerk took me to the back room in search of more. As we went, I prayed that God would give me what I needed for $20. We found more, but they were damaged and very dirty. He picked the best two, which had small nicks in them.

"How much for them?" I asked.

"Dirt and all, how about $20 for both?"

I bought them, and it confirmed to me that God does care. We shouldn't reach out to Him just when we need something, but be talking to Him daily.

A neighbor once told me she wouldn't bother God with requests like the ones I've mentioned. She said God had more important things to do than listen to my pleas, especially if I could handle the problems on my own. I think God cares about everything we do. I've found that when I don't submit decisions to Him, things don't go very well for me. In Matthew 10:30, Jesus says the very hairs of our head are numbered. If He knows and cares that much about me, I want to stay in tune with Him and watch as He works on my behalf.

Turn your eyes upon Jesus

The news rocked our church in Clintonville, Pennsylvania. Our dear pastor Rev. Lee Thompson had a stroke and was hospitalized. We all prayed for his recovery, but the elders had to move quickly to find lay preachers to fill the pulpit there and at two other churches where he pastored.

One Sunday morning after I arrived for worship, I heard the Lord say, "You're going to be asked to speak at the three churches." Instantly, I knew my subject—looking to Jesus based on Hebrews 12:1-14. So Monday evening I was not surprised when the phone rang, and I was asked to speak the next Sunday.

The writer of Hebrews compares the Christian life to a race. An athlete removes all excess clothing and weight so he or she can run well. Hebrews 12:1 says, "...let us lay aside every weight, and the sin that doth so easily beset us, and let us run with patience the race that is set before us."

In the Greek sprint races, the eye of the runner was trained and fixed upon the finish line. In our spiritual race of life, we must likewise keep our eyes fixed on Jesus.

An example of what happens when we take our eyes off Jesus is in Matthew 14:22-36. Jesus was walking on water, and He invited Peter to step out of the boat and come to Him. Peter had no trouble walking on water until his eyes shifted to the wind and the waves. Then he began to sink.

We are not to look to people or circumstances. We are to keep our eyes on Him. Don't be discouraged as Elijah was when Queen

Jezebel threatened to kill him in retribution for destroying the false prophets of Baal on Mt. Carmel (1 Kings 18). He ran away and asked God to take his life. Good thing God doesn't answer all our prayers! Instead God sent an angel to feed and encourage him. This man who had slain hundreds of false prophets fled from the idle threat of one woman.

As we live the Christian life, we can't win the race set before us in our own strength. We need to be emptied of self and filled with the Holy Spirit, to look always to Jesus, "the author and finisher of our faith" (Hebrews 12:2). He gives the victory. As Paul writes in Galatians 2:20: "I am crucified with Christ: nevertheless I live; yet not I, but Christ liveth in me: and the life which I now live in the flesh I live by the faith of the Son of God, who loved me, and gave Himself for me."

That wasn't all the sermon, but it was the most important part. We also sang the great hymn, *Turn Your Eyes Upon Jesus*, because it so expresses the heart of this message. The chorus proclaims:

Turn your eyes upon Jesus,
Look full in His wonderful face,
And the things of earth will grow strangely dim,
In the light of His glory and grace.

Correctional School for Boys

One door opens another when God is leading,
and you are available to Him.

I stood facing an assembly of 200 boys, along with school-teachers and staff at the George Junior Republic, a private correctional school for boys in nearby Grove City, Pennsylvania. I had just been introduced to this large assembly, and felt some stomach butterflies as I began to speak. It hit me then that this time was very special, and I would never forget it.

This was the Boys' Correctional School that had donated the X-ray machine to the mission hospital. After my tour to Ecuador, I received a phone call from one of the school staff asking me if I would teach a Sunday school lesson to the whole school in the main auditorium.

I did not hesitate. "Yes! I am always available to share with others about the goodness of God."

However, once I hung up the phone, I thought to myself, *These boys are not attending a regular school. They have been sent there for disciplinary reasons. What can I possibly tell them? What should I teach them about? How will they respond?*

These questions ran through my head. Knowing it is important to seek God in these matters, I asked Him to show me His message for these young people. No sooner did I ask, than I received the text I was to share. I was to tell these boys the story of Daniel in the den of lions.

That night I turned to the sixth chapter of Daniel and began studying the story of the courageous exile in Babylon. Daniel not only stood up for his beliefs and was willing to die for his faith, but he faced the lions with poise. God wanted me to encourage these boys to stand up to the lions in their lives – lions of slander, peer pressure, unfair criticism, accusations, failures, even illness... And I was to declare that they could do it with poise just like Daniel, if they put their faith in God.

The following Sunday morning, there I was. As I stepped up to the platform, the silence was so strong I could hear my own heart beating. To my amazement, the boys were alert and attentive. I began to tell the story, and the whole time I spoke, one could hear a pin drop. It was hard for me to believe that these boys were in a correctional facility. They were so well behaved.

The message I shared flowed out of God's Word and into the ears of these boys. Only the Lord knows what was going on in their heads and hearts as I spoke, but I suspected many felt alone and endangered like Daniel.

"Just imagine with me," I told them, "being thrown into a cold, dark, damp cave with wild lions who voraciously ate anything thrown at them."

No one moved or spoke in the audience. I hoped they could visualize this scene in their minds and understand the importance of trusting in God so much they could even face death for Him. I was praying they would be able to grasp the message of Daniel, who the Lord saved by shutting the mouths of these beasts. I prayed they would see God's involvement in answering prayer and the effect it had on all who witnessed this event, even King Darius.

To this day, I still marvel that I was given this opportunity. In my mind, I can still see some of the faces of those boys. I know

God had His reason for me being there that Sunday many years ago. As I prayed for them, it is with the hope that some of the boys' lives were turned around and changed. By faith, I have to believe that this is what happened.

Isaiah 55:11 says, "So shall My word be that goeth forth out of My mouth; it shall not return unto Me void, but it shall accomplish that which I please, and it shall prosper in the thing whereto I send it."

God and the tractor

Anyone visiting our place in Pennsylvania would quickly conclude that my husband Fred had a love for mechanical things in general and antique tractors in particular. Our coffee table and shelves were often covered in tractor books and magazines.

This interest came early in life. Fred's father, Newell Chase, owned a 1935 Cletrac model E 38 made in Cleveland, Ohio. This beauty was equipped with a winch specially designed for his work in the oil fields.

Fred grew up in Titusville, Pennsylvania, the location of the world's first successful oil well, drilled in 1859 and named for Edwin Drake. Although the Drake Well was shut down by the time Fred was born, the area still had many producing oil wells. When Fred's father no longer used the tractor in his work, Fred asked to purchase it.

"No, I think your brother, Rodger, might need it," he replied.

Newell Chase died in 1982, but it wasn't until Fred retired in 1987, that he wondered what happened to the tractor. He asked Rodger about it, only to learn it had been given to a man named Jim Huff. Fred couldn't get that tractor out of his mind so one day he paid a visit to Jim in Clintonville. Jim had sent it out for repairs several years ago, but the cost of the repair was too high. Jim had never paid the bill or picked it up from the shop.

When Fred learned this, he headed to the garage right away. There he discovered the rusted tractor in an area overgrown with weeds and high grass. To his dismay, it had not only had been

stripped of parts, but someone had poked holes in the radiator. After locating the tractor, he asked the mechanic if he could redeem it. The mechanic was willing to release it if the original bill was paid. Fred paid it right then, and hired someone to have it hauled to our home. This is such a reflection of Jesus, he locates us in all our damaged condition and redeems us.

What followed was a summer of tractor restoration, with sanding, painting and repairs that drew upon all of Fred's skills as a machinist. He even made missing parts. One mechanical challenge for him was the manifold. "It's in rough shape but I think I can get some life out of it," he said.

By the fall of 2000, he had built a nice metal shed with a cement floor to house our beautiful antique and to protect it from the elements. For years he enjoyed tinkering with it there.

In 2009 Fred's health was declining, and he began to think about selling the tractor. "I'm not sure what price to ask for it," he said.

"Let's ask the Lord," I suggested.

So we prayed about it. God impressed both of us with the asking price of $5,000. Fred contacted our friend, Bill Kline, who ran a farm equipment business. He agreed to advertise it on the internet, but without the price.

As soon as Ray Ethridge of Chappell Hill, Texas, saw the picture he asked about buying it. Before hearing our price, Ray made an offer of $5,000. We took this as confirmation and agreed. When Ray said the check would be in tomorrow's mail, Fred began to be concerned about the old manifold.

At this point, we still did not realize how rare this tractor was. I called an antique parts dealer in Eastern Pennsylvania, and the man politely informed me it would be next to impossible to find. "This particular manifold was only made for a few tractors and was never reproduced," he said. "But give me your phone number, and we'll see if something turns up."

I told Fred, "God knows where the part is." We went to prayer and put the problem in God's hands. Using Fred's many tractor magazines and books, I started again to call places that sold parts. These men were not so polite. One said, "Good luck lady....

Fred with his labor of love – a restored 1935 Cletrac model E 38

Ha! Ha! Ha!" None offered to take my phone number. They let me know my search was hopeless.

Meanwhile, Fred decided to try to repair the manifold himself. He came in early for lunch one day so we could drive to town and buy necessary materials for the job. Unknown to us, God had already reached across our country to locate the manifold. As we were eating lunch the phone rang, and I heard the voice of that first parts dealer, Eli Zimmerman, (the only one who took our number).

"Do you still want that manifold?"

I yelled, "YES!" so loudly it must have hurt his ear. He told us that shortly after I had called him, he had another call from a man in California. This man told Eli he was dismantling an old tractor and wanted to sell the parts. As soon as the seller described the manifold, Eli knew it was just what we were looking for, and he bought the box of parts.

Eli had waited until he had the box in hand to examine the manifold before calling us. God's timing is so very amazing! Fred and I rejoiced even more when we had the part in our hands and discovered it was in mint condition. Fred presented the buyer with a 75-year-old tractor in perfect working order.

The Kona Years

No time for retirement

Trust in the LORD with all your heart and lean not on
your own understanding. In all your ways acknowledge Him,
and He shall direct your paths (Proverbs 3:5-6, NKJV).

When we first visited Hawaii in 1967, we fell in love with the
islands and the people. It was a dream vacation for us, but back
then I could never have imagined that God would bring us back
there for His purposes.

After Fred retired in 1989, we decided to vacation there again
to escape the harsh winter in Pennsylvania. While walking on
Waikiki Beach one day I asked: "Why don't we come to Hawaii
for the winter?"

"I see no reason not to come back," Fred agreed.

So for the next two years we "wintered" on the island of Oahu,
just relaxing and basking in the warm sunshine. In March of
1992, we attended a service at the Chinese Church in Honolulu.
The speaker was Paul Hawkins, a leader of the Youth With A
Mission (YWAM) base in Kona, on the Big Island of Hawaii. He
gave a great message and told about YWAM's work in Kona. We
wanted to meet him so we hung around after the service.

"So what are you doing here in Hawaii?" he asked.

"We're just relaxing mostly," I replied.

"We could sure use your help in Kona. We're building out
our University of the Nations, and we have a volunteer program

called Mission Builders. I'll send you an application."

Paul took our address and sure enough, an application came in the mail. We completed it and were accepted for the following October. Mission Builders pay their own airfare to get to Kona, then receive room and board while working in construction or various departments on campus. Most serve for one to three months. Over three decades, this program has given thousands of Christians a wonderful opportunity to contribute their time and expertise to world missions.

That October marked the beginning of a new adventure in God for us. We have come back every winter for over 20 years. There are so many God stories from my time at the University of the Nations.

One thing I love most about the campus is the opportunity it gives to interact with people from all over the world. One of those was Xenia Konig, a YWAMer who was serving on staff there when I met her in 1995. During our conversation, she mentioned they had a condo they wanted to rent out for a few months while they went to the mainland to be with their two daughters. It was necessary for them financially to have someone renting out their condo during this time or they would not be able to make the trip at all.

In the book of Nehemiah 1:2, I read about the encounter that Nehemiah had with Hanani when he learned from him about the condition of walls of Jerusalem that needed repair. I have learned from this and other life situations, the importance of knowing that nothing in our path is ever an accident. Because of this encounter, Nehemiah heard of the disrepair of Jerusalem's walls and played a key role in seeing them rebuilt. Take it to the Lord in prayer was a key role in Nehemiah's life. His first reaction and impulse was always to pray.

94

When I returned to our living quarters at the Mission Builder housing facility, I told Fred about my conversation with Xenia. We then prayed together for them and that God would help them in this time of need.

We felt God speaking these words to our heart: "Go ahead and bless Nick and Xenia!" So, I obediently went to the Konigs and said we would rent their condo during the winter months of 1995 and 1996. They were overjoyed to hear that someone wanted to rent their place for the five months they would be gone. We were happy too, and it was a joy to stay in their lovely condo during their absence.

My job on campus was not an easy one. I served as the Head of Housekeeping at the Global Outreach Center and had 10 persons to supervise. I didn't just assign the volunteers the jobs, I was out there cleaning and scrubbing and training them in their tasks. It was hard work physically, especially at my age.

One day, as I was cleaning and praying, I said to God, "Lord, how can I get an easier job around here?" Just two days later, Xenia approached me and said to me, "Since you will be renting my condominium, you should also take over my job here!"

Xenia was working in the Office of Public Relations with Ken Clewett. I looked upwards and silently thanked God for opening this door for me to work in an office and as assistant to one of the busiest people on campus. Once again God was showing me His faithfulness in hearing and answering prayer. Xenia never went back to work for Ken Clewett. I ended up being his assistant for 12 years.

When we got back to Pennsylvania in the spring, Fred and I each had 35,000 frequent-flyer miles. I called United Airlines' frequent-flyer program to begin the process of booking our return flight to Hawaii in November or December, our winter months. I was informed each time, "There are no seats available using frequent-flyer miles during those months." Booking a flight can only be done 11 months in advance, and it must also be ticketed 30 days before departure.

When I was booking our flights home from Hawaii, I had called in the month of May and the first departure date the airlines gave me then was for a flight leaving on January 29th.

Now, to book our flights back to Kona, the date I chose was November 15th or 16th. I continued to pray and put it all in God's hands while faithfully doing my part to call in regularly, to check for any available seats for an earlier date.

Fred was more doubtful and also more impatient. One day after hearing me dial United Airlines for the umpteenth time, he got exasperated and yelled out to me, "Ruth, get off that telephone, and just go ahead and pay for our tickets!"

Thirty days went by and one night, as I was studying for my Bible class, I heard God say to me, "Call the airlines!"

Whenever I talked to the airline agents, I gave them multiple options to apply our frequent-flyer points. "It's okay if you can get us to any other of the islands," I said. That didn't seem to help. No flights were available during that time period, even to other islands.

This time, when I dialed the toll-free number, the agent took a long time researching the flights. Finally, she said we could fly to Maui but I would have to pay for the extra interisland airfare hop to the Big Island. It would also necessitate a hotel stay on Maui as our flight would arrive too late to catch the last flight out to Kona. Altogether, it would cost about $150 in airfare for the two of us, plus hotel expenses.

I had been calling for months, and this was the first glimmer of hope for us to use our frequent-flyer miles. But after taking our names and frequent-flyer account numbers, she told me that for some reason, Fred and I had not been credited for some of our miles. Fred did not need these miles for this flight, but I did. The agent said, "Could you please send in some documentation to validate that you took these flights and earned these miles?"

I asked for an extension to book the flight but she said it was not possible. I then asked to speak with a supervisor.

Moments later, I was speaking with a United Airlines supervisor who after hearing of my dilemma asked me a question that surprised me. He just came out and asked me if I was a Christian.

"Yes, yes I am." He told me that he too was a believer.

"Somehow I always find myself getting involved with Christians having flight difficulties."

When I picked up the phone to dial the 1-800 number, I could have been connected with any of 5,000 United Airlines agents, but God had me speak to this particular man. We both knew this was no coincidence.

He checked out flights available and said to me, "You are not entitled to the seats given you to fly to Maui, but I am opening up seats for you to fly directly to the Keahole airport in Kailua-Kona. However, you will have a stopover in San Francisco where you will have to spend the night." He also offered us some half-price vouchers to use on a hotel stay there.

Oh my, I thought. *This is going to save us a lot of money not having to pay for the flight from Maui to Kona.* I was thrilled with this help from above and was praising God!

The next day, we got a call from this supervisor who informed us that our frequent-flyer miles would now be credited on my account, and he would debit the amount needed for the flight.

I thought of the verse in Ephesians 3:20 that says, "Now unto Him that is able to do exceedingly abundantly above all that we ask or think..." God once again did the impossible as I did the possible in calling and praying. This amounted to a savings of $1,200 in airfare. I said to the Lord, "God this is not our money. We give it back to you. We are willing to share this money with someone else who has a need for it."

It was not long before we found some important needs in our community, such as a man who was dying of cancer. We gave him $500. Another couple we heard about were unable to pay their rent that month, and so we gave them $500. We were thrilled to be able to meet these needs through these extra funds. Finally, we prayed and felt we were to give an extra amount of $200 to a young missionary we were already supporting but who needed extra funds for a mission trip. There was the $1,200.

We knew it was God's will we come to Hawaii, and we arrived November 15, thanking and praising God. We knew it was His divine intervention that caused our flight to be changed from Pittsburgh to San Francisco instead of Maui. Had we left on the 15th, our flight would have been cancelled because a big snow storm closed the airport. By leaving on the 14th, we avoided the storm, had a good night's rest in San Francisco, and did some sightseeing. We got to see the Golden Gate Bridge and had a delightful ride over the hills on the city's famous trolley car (cable car).

Oh what a mighty God we serve!

God's name change intervention

When I was 37-years-old, I began to pursue my life-long dream to visit to the Holy Land. One day I said to my Mom, "I need to get a birth certificate."

"Well," she said, "You were born at home, and I am not sure your birth was even registered. If they do find you have one, don't expect to see the name of Ruth on it because I never gave the doctor that name."

I contacted the Department of Vital Statistics in Pennsylvania and asked if there were any records of my birth on September 16, 1928. To my relief, the doctor attending my mother for my delivery had registered my birth in Forest County. They sent me a certified copy of my birth record. But as Mom had said, my name Ruth was nowhere to be found on the birth registry.

Throughout all my growing up years, I was called Ruth so I asked Mom why I was called Darlulia on the birth record. Mom said she changed my name to Ruth because my siblings couldn't pronounce Darlulia. After repeating the pronunciation to them over and over again, she gave up and started calling me Ruth. No one had trouble saying Ruth.

When I finally got my passport application processed, the name inside and under my photo was Darlulia with no middle name at all. This concerned me since the name on my school records, job applications, Social Security card, driver's license and even my marriage certificate all said Ruth. But I didn't act on this until Fred and I began wintering in Hawaii.

In the spring of 2013, when I was 84 years old, I went to apply for a Hawaii state identification card. When I talked to the Department of Motor Vehicles, they told me that I needed to supply them with my birth certificate, my marriage license and several other documents. I decided this was the time to officially change my name so the birth certificate matched my other important papers and documents.

To get the new birth certificate, I first contacted a lawyer in Pennsylvania. He told me that he could have my name officially changed for a fee of $1,709.39. I was appalled. I told God that I would rather give that money to a missionary to do the Lord's work.

So, I contacted another lawyer, and he was willing to charge me just $1,000 for the name change fee. I was still hesitant to put out that much money. When I thought about it some more, I had an impression in my mind to contact the Lt. Governor's Office in Hawaii. When I did this, I found out that if I processed my request through his office, the charge would be just $200. I was in Pennsylvania at the time so I quickly called a friend in Hawaii to assist me in getting the necessary forms.

As I read through the instructions and requisites, I discovered I would be required to have a current copy of my birth certificate that was dated no more than 90 days before beginning the process. I then thought of my friend Becky who worked for the state House of Representatives and had helped Fred and me in previous times when we needed assistance with state matters. Becky helped by contacting a woman who worked in the division of Vital Records. She asked us, "Wasn't your husband Fred military?"

"Yes, he served in the armed forces."

"Well, if Fred is a veteran there is no charge for this name change."

Praise the Lord! She proceeded to make the needed corrections and provided me with two updated certified copies of my birth records. The State had changed my name and birth record at no cost.

This is particularly significant now because, at 84 years of age, all my important papers and legal documents are in the name of Ruth Darlulia Chase. If I had passed away before seeing to it that the name of Ruth was added to my birth certificate, it may have been quite difficult to settle my estate.

But that's not the end of the story. Remember the $1709.39 the first lawyer wanted to charge me? I told God then that I would rather give it to a missionary doing God's work. Well God remembered!

Not long after this, I met a woman who was praying and trusting God to provide money to go on a mission trip. I asked her how much she needed and when she told me $1,706, I laughed. I did not need to pray to know that this was a "God-led" situation and a time to give. The extra $3.39 covered the postage I needed to get the paperwork from Hawaii.

God works in mysterious and interesting ways! Nothing ever takes the Lord by surprise. It might surprise us, but not God. We need to trust Him completely.

Christmas parade challenge

What an honor, privilege and blessing to serve God at University of the Nations in Kailua Kona, Hawaii, where staff, students and Mission Builders (volunteers) come from all over the world.

Our Mission Builder coordinator at the time, Glen Roper, challenged our group, "Would anyone here be willing to help build a float for the Kona Christmas parade?" Only four raised their hands to volunteer, so Glen decided to drop the project. The parade was to be held on December 16th.

Somehow, I had a hard time shaking off this opportunity for a local outreach. One morning I woke up after having a vision in my dreams of the whole world. Then, I heard the voice of God speak to my heart, "Do the float!" Just like that, I also received the theme for the float: "The Cradle To The Cross For The World."

At our next Mission Builder meeting, I told our fellow volunteers I felt God wanted me to take on this project. "If anyone else is interested in building this Christmas float, please come to Room 8A at Hale Ola," which was our housing at the time. "We have only one and a half weeks to work on this before the date of the parade so we need all the help we can get."

One thing I have learned through the years is if we attempt to do something for God, Satan will oppose and seek to stop it. My own husband told me, "You are opening a can of worms that Glen Roper closed, you know." The enemy can use even those closest to us to bring discouragement.

That night, both Fred and I were delighted when 14 people showed up to volunteer. We knew God had raised up the right team to build the float. Staff member Paul Pittenridge obtained a four-wheel wagon frame to use for our float base. He and Fred and another man then put down four sheets of 4'x8' plywood to give the float a strong platform and expand it to 8'x16'. We located a piece of carpet and fastened this over the plywood sheets. Next came an eight-foot wooden cross that we bolted on the back end of the trailer. On the cross we hung some grave cloths and a flower lei. I asked Molly Young, a Hawaiian woman representing our host nation, to sit at the foot of the cross.

I wondered what could be used to represent the world. Then I thought of the globe located in U of N's GO Center auditorium. It was made of fitted stained glass pieces created to form a world that lit up from the inside. It had been a gift given to YWAM founders Loren and Darlene Cunningham. I knew I needed to get special permission to borrow this for the parade. With fear and trembling, I prayerfully approached Rick Sorum, who was leading the Crossroads Discipleship Training School there and responsible for the auditorium.

"May I please use the lighted globe in your classroom for the YWAM Christmas parade float?" I asked.

He could probably hear the hesitancy in my voice, but he smiled and said, "I have no problem with that." Once again, I recognized the hand of God leading us step by step.

The world globe was attached to a wooden box that is three-feet square. We wrapped the base in gold foil paper with bright red ribbon tied around it. We knew this wrapped box with the globe on top represented God's gift to the world.

On the four corners of the large display we placed four red

covered stools decorated with a floral garland at the base. We decided to have four people representing the various races – red, yellow, black and white. Representing the Asian races was Kye Suk Lee a young Korean who wore her traditional Korean dress. Representing the black race, we had Sherrell Daniels who wore a lovely red-and-orange-colored dress. Terina Bracy, as the white model, wore a Dutch costume with a little blue apron, wooden shoes, and a crisp white hat. Sonia Hurtado, dressed in Mexican Indian attire was chosen to represent the Indian nations. She donned a red-and-white flowered dress and wore red flowers in her black hair.

We wanted to portray the true meaning of Christmas of course, so we included a nativity with a wooden manger. Staff members Brian and Roxanne Hickey dressed as Mary and Joseph, holding their 26-day-old infant "Jesus" in their arms. Their other two children played the part of shepherds.

We painted large banners on each side of the float, with the message, "God So Loved the World."

On the other side of the float was the Bethlehem star that

shone in the darkness over the holy family. A pick-up truck was used to haul the float and its occupants. Marching in front of the float entry were two young men, Brian Augat and Ben Hewett, who carried a large banner announcing our campus entry, "University of the Nations." It gave me such joy to see this colorful representation of God's love for the nations and to hear Christmas music from the cab of the pickup truck as it eased past a multitude of people lining both sides of Ali'i Drive. The sun was setting over Kona just then but the Son was rising in many hearts.

"Be anxious for nothing," the Bible says in Philippians 4:6 (NKJV). I must confess that I did go through some anxious mo-

ments while waiting for the Monday morning paper to arrive announcing the winners. Not only had University of the Nations taken First Place, but we also were given a trophy and a $25 check.

In reflecting on that experience, I was reminded again of the story of Nehemiah. He was obedient when God called him to build the wall of Jerusalem. The Lord tells us in His Word, "To obey is better than sacrifice" (1 Samuel 15:22). When God is building something, there is always opposition. Nehemiah met opposition with faith and trust in God – and hard work.

When we started building the Christmas float, some said there wasn't enough time to complete it. One Mission Builder complained, "You are giving us a lot of work to do here." When given use of the stained glass globe, some had tried to discourage us saying it would not be wise. How could we replace it if we broke it? My prayer at the time was, "God, you gave us the world [globe], now will you protect it please? I had perfect peace over its care.

I believe the Lord put together our small band of workers for that Christmas float. We prayed together, worked together and grew in unity and faith.

Isaiah 26:3 says, "Thou wilt keep him in perfect peace, whose mind is stayed on Thee: because he trusteth in Thee." Through faith, hard work, and the Word of the Lord, Nehemiah and his workers completed construction of the two-mile wall in only 52 days. What an outstanding accomplishment. Even the heathen had to admit the wall was a work of God.

This was the first float we worked on for the annual Christmas Parade in Kailua-Kona. Fred and I ended up doing a meaningful Christmas float every year for the next 14 years, from 1995 to 2009. Many of these floats won first or second place in the float entries. I made sure we always included a nativity scene and portrayed the true meaning of Christmas. We prayed the Lord would speak to people along the parade route of God's love and goodness.

We appreciated the honor of winning cash prizes and trophies, but the real purpose was presenting the love of God to all. This project belonged to God and He worked a miracle in and through us. Praise His Holy Name!

For unto you is born this day in the city of David a Savior, which is Christ the LORD (Luke 2:11).

Battling Cancer

Living in Hawaii has many benefits, but the tropical sun takes its toll on those of us with fair skin. Most physicians in Hawaii are quite familiar with it, but not so those in our home state.

In June 2009, Fred had surgery to remove cancer in his right ear. A few weeks after the surgery, we noticed the ear lobe had a lesion and was discharging a brown liquid. Eventually it healed. I described this discharge-and-heal cycle to his dermatologist, Dr. Dunagin, as it continued into September and October. Dr. Dunagin examined it and said, "Looks good to me." So we left for our annual time as volunteers at the University of the Nations in Kailua Kona, Hawaii. All through the winter months the discharge cycle continued, and we grew more concerned and frustrated.

Back home, we saw Dr. Dunagin once again. He still insisted, "His ear looks good to me." I protested, "There is a brown discharge that reoccurs." He finally agreed to do a biopsy "just to satisfy you." Ten days later a letter came confirming that it was cancer, and we needed to see a Mohs[2] (skin cancer) doctor. We contacted L & B Skin Cancer & Mohs Surgery Center in Pittsburgh.

Fred was scheduled for surgery on October 5. That seemed

---

2   Today, Mohs surgery is accepted as the single most effective technique for removing Basal Cell and Squamous Cell carcinoma, the two most common skin cancers. It spares the greatest amount of healthy tissue while also most completely expunging cancer cells; cure rates are an unparalleled 98 percent or higher with Mohs.

far off, so we trusted God for an earlier surgery date. I made a follow-up call with questions and asked the receptionist if Fred could get an earlier surgery date. God heard our prayers for she had just received a cancellation for the next day, September 15, with the head surgeon, Dr. David Brodland. He is actually an instructor for the micro-surgery Mohs technique. God gave us the best surgeon possible!

The morning of the surgery Dr. Brodland remarked, "I hope I can save the ear." He worked from 8 a.m. to 6 p.m. that day to remove the cancer and reconstruct Fred's ear. The surgery was a success, but it left Fred with a smaller ear and no lobe.

We had to return to Dr. Dunagin to have the bandages changed before returning to Hawaii. He noted, "I see Fred had some surgery."

"Yes, they were able to save his ear—no thanks to you. The next time your patient speaks, listen!" Unfortunately, that was not Fred's last encounter with cancer. The very same month of

Fred kept working in the UofN woodshop despite his cancer.

Fred's ear surgery, I noticed a small dark spot on his left lower eyelid. It caused me some concern so I called for an appointment at the Laurel Eye Clinic near our home in Pennsylvania. We would soon be returning to Hawaii, and I wanted to get it checked out before we left. The doctor examined it, and said he saw no problem. He told us to wash the eyelid everyday with soap and warm water. Over the next few months, that small thing became a growth. Sometimes when I washed the eyelid, the growth would fall off but it always returned. Now even more concerned, I made an eye appointment in Hawaii.

The doctor remarked, "It looks like skin cancer and will require a plastic surgeon who is an eyelid specialist." Fred also was seen by a local oncologist who said, "You need an eyelid specialist." There was one in Honolulu, but we decided to wait until we returned to Pennsylvania.

Arriving home in May, 2010, we went back to the local eye doctor. He wanted to give us salve to treat the problem. I nearly exploded.

"Two doctors in Hawaii told him it's skin cancer and said he needs an eyelid specialist. I want to know where there is one."

"There is a clinic at Wexford, near Pittsburgh, but it's not easy to get in."

The earliest appointment we could get was June 22. I prayed for a cancellation because Fred was about to start a new medication for his multiple myeloma, and I felt he should have surgery before starting it. I called about cancellations, but there were none. The secretary said, "There is no waiting list, you need to keep calling."

The next week God said to me, "Call Wexford."

The clinic's head surgeon, Dr. David Buerger, had a cancellation June 1. I booked it immediately. Dr. Buerger's office staff said the earliest he could do the eyelid surgery was July 19. Once again I trusted God. Fred had the physical for his surgery on June 2.

That same day I heard God say, "Call the surgical department about waiting to start the new medication."

As a result of that call they changed Fred's surgery date to June 21, the day before he was to have had his first office visit with Dr. Buerger. The surgery showed the growth to be an ulcerated Basosquamos carcinoma which had both basal cells and squamous cells. The surgery saved Fred's eyelid. I am deeply grateful for the surgeons' skill and wisdom, but also to God for opening the way so he could be treated before it grew worse. What an awesome God we serve!

I needed God's help for my own medical needs the next few years. In March 2011, I noticed a sore in my right ear. I put antiseptic salve on it, but it never healed. I was scheduled to have cataract surgery on my right eye. I had a physical for the surgery, but my doctor didn't pay any attention when I told him about my ear. I had my surgery, and during a follow-up appointment the eye doctor asked,

"How long have you had that sore in your ear."

"Several months," I replied.

"It looks like cancer. You need to see a dermatologist soon."

It's pretty bad when your eye doctor has to tell you that you have cancer in your ear.

I heeded his advice and called a Mohs doctor in Butler, PA. I was scheduled for surgery at the end of September. Thinking it would be no big deal, I didn't pray about getting an earlier date. How I wish I had. During the weeks I was waiting, the cancer spread. My doctor started surgery at 1 p.m. and finished at 8:15 p.m. He had to go into the ear five times and then do a skin graft. Afterward I had an infection that forced me to postpone my annual flight to Hawaii.

I learned the hard way. When we don't pray about things like this, we are trusting in our own wisdom. God always knows best. I wouldn't make the same mistake two years later when I got another skin cancer. It began with a scab in my hair at the left temple. I would pick at it until the scab came off, but then it would return. Right before I left for our winter trip to Hawaii, my hairdresser Becky, said, "You need to see a dermatologist. When a sore doesn't heal and doesn't hurt, I've learned it's cancer."

I made an appointment to see a Mohs doctor. A biopsy was taken and the result was cancer. On September 19, I was told there were no openings for surgery available before I was scheduled to fly to Hawaii on October 18. I remembered God answering prayer for Fred's eyelid surgery and cancer of the ear and my mistake in 2011 for ear surgery. Nothing is impossible with God.

Once again I prayed for a cancellation. I called the scheduling department Monday, September 22 and was told the schedule was booked full. So I asked to transfer my call to another department. The woman who answered the phone was in the room when I had my biopsy. She said she couldn't promise she could help me, but would try. She was able to work me in between patients on October 2. I still was rejoicing an hour later the phone rang. I was told they could operate on me the next day. I had surgery on September 23, which gave me a month to heal before going away for the winter. What an awesome God!

Two miracles of healing

Summon your might, O God. Display your power,
O God, as you have in the past (Psalm 68:28, NLT).

We got up at our regular 6 a.m., but that Sunday morning in 2009 wasn't typical at all. We'd usually be getting ready for church, but Fred hadn't slept well so he decided to return to bed for more rest.

It was after 10 a.m. when he joined me in the kitchen, and I started making pancakes. Fred seemed his usual self, but when he went to the refrigerator for milk, I heard the crash of his cup falling to the floor. Fred just stood there, staring into space.

"Fred! Fred!" I shouted.

No response.

I turned off the stove and tried to shake him. Still no response.

Right away I knew he was having a stroke and called 911. While on the phone, Fred stumbled toward the table and collapsed into a chair.

When the paramedics arrived and loaded Fred into the ambulance, I climbed in up front. I felt concerned but not afraid. God had been so good to us, how could I not trust Him now? I prayed, "Lord, I'm expecting a miracle, just like You did for him in Kona." In that moment, God filled my heart with peace. As Isaiah 26:3 says, "Thou wilt keep him in perfect peace, whose mind is stayed on Thee: because he trusteth in Thee."

As the ambulance raced with sirens screaming for those 28 miles to the hospital, I glanced out the window and noticed the brilliant fall colors of the Pennsylvania countryside. Suddenly I realized this was the very day we had planned to fly to Hawaii. There were no seats available so we had to delay our return to Kona by a week. If we had left on this date, Fred likely would have been in the air when the stroke occurred.

The United Presbyterian Medical Center had established a stroke unit just two years earlier. Fred became the 70th patient to be treated there. When we arrived at the hospital, they hurried to do a CAT scan. They had to locate the blood clot that caused the stroke. If they could treat it in time, they could save him from the most debilitating effects of the stroke.

The staff was scrambling as fast as they could, and everyone looked tense.

The head nurse noticed how calm I was and thought I didn't understand what was happening.

"Don't you know this is a trauma?" she asked.

"Yes I know."

She hurried off, but the question gave me an opportunity to testify to a young blonde attendant who had overheard the conversation. She had also seen Fred's condition. He arrived there unresponsive, unable to communicate, almost lifeless.

"I am trusting God to heal my husband, just like he did four years ago."

I began to recount to her what had transpired in Hawaii in December of 2005. I found Fred shaking uncontrollably and took him to the Kona hospital. He was diagnosed with double pneumonia and streptococcus infection. With his blood pressure at 60, he was rushed to the ICU.

"Fred was at the point of death. I called our friends and family to pray for his healing. And God miraculously healed him. By Monday, Fred was put in a regular room. On Tuesday, the doctor visited him and said, 'You are doing remarkably well, Mr. Chase.'

"By Thursday – just six days after he was rushed to the ICU – he was discharged. Two doctors stood shaking their heads, and one said, 'I've never seen anyone so close to death who didn't die.'

"The next day Fred was helping work on a float for the Christmas parade, and the following Monday he went back to work. It was a miracle, and that's why I'm trusting God for his healing now."

The CAT scan showed the blood clot that caused the stroke was lodged in the temporal lobe of Fred's brain. A specialist advised me that Fred was a good candidate for a clot-busting drug called Tissue Plasminogen Activator (TPA). The drug had to be administered within three hours of the stroke, and Fred was still in that window of time.

The doctor lifted up my dear husband's arm, and it fell limp. Then he lifted his legs, and they also were lifeless.

"Mrs. Chase, your husband is a candidate for the TPA but it could possibly cause a fatal hemorrhage. Do we have your permission to use the TPA clot buster?"

I looked over at Fred who was lying on the table, looking as lifeless as a corpse.

"Yes, go ahead."

The head nurse immediately administered the drug, and we collectively held our breath to see what effect it would have. Within minutes Fred began to speak. Then he moved his right leg, crossing it over the left one.

"Did you see what he just did!" the nurse shouted. Everyone

in the room got excited. One by one, all the physical signs of the stroke injury dissipated.

In the ICU they asked Fred to read a written article and to identify objects from pictures. He easily passed both tests. By Monday he was transferred to a regular room.

The blonde, blue-eyed young woman I'd talked to earlier came by a couple of days later. When she saw Fred, she threw up her hands and cried out, "Amazing! Absolutely amazing for an 84-year-old man to recover like this!"

The stroke had injured the temporal lobe of the brain, which regulates the speech, understanding and know-how of the body. But Fred was able to walk and talk quite normally. The young woman asked for permission to do a story about the miraculous recovery she had witnessed. And of course, we agreed.

The usual treatment for stroke victims is physical therapy, and that's what the doctor advised. But at the rehab center, Fred told them he didn't need therapy. "How do you rehabilitate an 84-year-old man anyway?" he asked. "I can walk and talk and eat. Can I just go home?"

So just like Kona, six days after the stroke he was sent home. Later that week, a physical therapist came by to check on him. He put Fred through a few more tests and declared, "You're right, Mr. Chase, you don't need my help."

That settled for the record what we already knew. The recovery was complete. God had healed my husband once again!

Losing the one you love

When Lee Thompson became our pastor and greeted us for the first time, he shook Fred's hand and said: "The other day someone told me, 'That Fred Chase is a real gentleman.'"

Fred just smiled and tried to deflect the attention. Yes, he was a gentleman, but he was so much more. He was a man of God. A faithful and loving husband. A loyal friend. A kind and helpful neighbor. A skilled and dedicated worker. A servant-hearted volunteer. A man who discipled others through his skills and lifestyle.

In our 62 years of marriage, I found him to be truthful, dependable, respectful, and a man of integrity. He built the new home we moved into when we got married (just like in the Jewish tradition). Most people today can't comprehend how he built our nice home in Clintonville, Pennsylvania, without a mortgage. But as one raised in the Depression, he hated debt, and he saved to buy the land and materials needed.

We never needed a repair man for the house. Fred would tackle almost anything. He said: "God gave you a brain so use it." And he did.

Fred was a machinist by trade and worked in Quality Control at Cooper Energy inspecting parts for making diesel engines. Every day when he went to work I would hand him his lunch pail and say: "Have a good day." He would reply: "Every day is a good day." Not once did he say he had a bad one.

He loved our home, and he spent much of his leisure time

there. He loved gardening and built a nursery where he cultivated his prized hybrid Day Lilies. He also built his own machine shop where he accumulated great mounds of spare parts and scrap metals. He never wasted anything he considered useful – even time.

He loved life and fought to live as his health declined. He survived bladder cancer surgery and a fall from the roof in 1985, cancer of the urethra in 1999; and multiple myeloma, which was first diagnosed in 2005. He endured over five years of chemotherapy without complaint. The only negative thing I ever heard him say was that it made his food "taste rotten."

Through all these surgeries and treatments, God still allowed us to continue to go and work at the University of the Nations in Kona. We thought that streak might end in 2010 when the doctor found cancer on Fred's eye lid and his ear. But God came through again. After successful surgeries we were able to go to Hawaii on schedule.

Fred lost his fight for life later that year. He was hospitalized three days with pneumonia and sepsis and died peacefully on

At the celebration of Fred's life with Pastor Kealoha Kaopua, Madge (Bridges) Pike, others.

December 4, 2010. His death rocked my world, but I clung to my unshakeable, loving God. In His mercy, He spared Fred from dying of the multiple myeloma, which is a painful death. If he had lived, the doctors likely would have placed Fred in a nursing home, something he never wanted.

On the night of Fred's death I prayed, "It's just you and me now, Lord. Please help me." I praised and thanked God for all the memorable years we had together. Fred was 85 years old.

I remembered my mum saying: "God promises to take care of the widow." And He sure has with me. I learned praise can lift the burden of grief, and God gave me wonderful peace.

There in Kona, I was surrounded by kind and supportive friends at the University of the Nations who put on a wonderful a memorial service for Fred on December 12, 2010. He was later buried in Grove City, PA.

Officiating at the service was Kahu (Pastor) Kealoha Kaopua, a leader of YWAM's Island Breeze Ministries. Fred's good friend and work supervisor Ed Pike gave the eulogy, and there was worship music by Jill Herringshaw and hula by Hero Wooching. I'm grateful to all those who honored Fred that day and supported

Friends viewed photos and Hero Wooching danced a beautiful hula at the UofN service.

me in the weeks that followed.

When I returned to Pennsylvania in May, one of my big concerns was what to do with all the things Fred had accumulated. God sent two kind and hard-working men to my rescue. With God's help these men emptied a two-stall, three-story garage full of metal and junk. They made 28 trips to the junkyard, each with a flatbed trailer load.

I also prayed about selling the country house Fred built when we first got married. But where would God want me to live? I asked God to sell the house and get me an apartment at the same time if He wanted me to move. This was a big decision, and I wanted no mistake. Several had asked about buying my house. One person wanted to buy it and said I could pay rent until I found an apartment. I said, "No way, not until I know where God is moving me will I sell."

One day I went to an area in Grove City where I had a Bible study for years. One of my students lived in the Filer Apartments across the street from the Bible study. That day I called to put my name on their waiting list. Isaiah 26:3 says, "Thou wilt keep him in perfect peace whose mind is stayed on Thee: because he trusteth in Thee."

I had perfect peace in waiting to make this important decision. I headed for Hawaii in the fall of 2011, my first time going there without Fred. So many memories swirled in my mind as I checked in at the Pittsburgh airport. I went through security, then took a tram to the departure area. Stepping onto the upward escalator, I had a small suitcase in one hand and a small carryon in the other. I looked down and part of my toe was on the other step. As it went up, it threw me backward, landing me flat on my back and head. People rushed to help me but I was just bruised a little. What a miracle I wasn't hurt! I grabbed my bags and got on the escalator properly and hurried to the gate.

I had another fruitful season serving God in the UofN Library, and returned to Pennsylvania in May 2012. There was much to do, and one day I decided to weed around my house while it was cool outside. As I was weeding, I heard God say, "Call the Filers." Right away I called Donna Filer. She said an apartment had just become available. Another woman rented it, then decided she didn't want it. I asked to rent it and called the woman who had asked to buy my house last summer. She still wanted it. Just as I had prayed, God arranged the sale of my house and the move to Grove City.

I now scrambled to move, selling or giving away the furnishings in the house. Over a six-week span, I sold many large and small items in a continuing garage sale. Most of my furniture pieces fit in my new apartment, but I decided to advertise for sale a wooden kitchen table with four chairs for $250.

The phone rang early the next morning. A woman asked how big the table was. I said, "It's 24-inches but it has two drop leaves. With those in place, it becomes a round table."

"I really need one like that. Our house burned down and we're moving into a small trailer house."

I gasped, "Mrs. Guiste is that you?"

"Yes. It is."

"Well, I will give you that table set."

I had heard their house had burned. Now God was giving me a chance to help meet their need.

When they came to load it, I told them I was a Christian and had prayed about helping them. Mike Guiste said he wasn't very religious. I told him I wasn't being religious. I explained that there are many religions, but only one plan of salvation through Jesus Christ. I trust every time they eat at that table, they will think about that and give their lives to the Lord.

I had never moved before but prayed, putting it all in God's hands. Every week my neighbor who visited his mother a short distance from my apartment, would take 10 or more packed boxes to my apartment. He then took all 34 of the drawers. He took the last ones a week before I moved in on July 23, 2012. My furniture was moved and placed. I was all settled in a couple of weeks. The Lord made it so easy.

Epilogue

I continue to go back and forth between Pennsylvania and Hawaii each year. I have many heart ties of family and friends in my native state, but I love my work and my home in Hawaii. I'm nearing 90 years of age, but I still feel at home in Youth With A Mission Kona. I have grown to love this place so much that I chose to make Hawaii my official state of residence in 2013, three years after Fred passed.

My life has been a wonderful journey, and I'm forever grateful to my awesome Father God. He is true to all of His promises.